Stefano Versace

American Ice Dream

MNAMON

CHAPTER 1. THE MADNESS OF PRODUCTION

*Dive into the right market without
waiting for the perfect circumstances.*

A flavor for you: champagne.
Properties: elegant taste activates enthusiasm and stimulates the love for details.

THE SPARK: WHEN EVERYTHING BEGAN

"Sorry, Dr. Versace. We understand how you feel but try to understand our situation; we must do something after all ... "This is the moment where it all began. A trivial phrase, repeated several times by the two health board officials. That very night they decided to come in for a routine check in my restaurant, rather than in one of the many other restaurants in Urbino. They had not found anything relevant- nothing irregular to report. But they still managed to draw up a statement with a fine of just over 250 Euros.

You pay for the lack of visibility of the 'No Smoking' sign.

Yes, I am referring to an old Italian law reminding citizens of its existence. The fact is this sentence of the health board would have sent anyone on a rampage. Can you imagine? What honest merchant in the neighborhood would have not been thrown into turmoil? Especially in 2013 when to survive with operating costs, seemingly increasing, in a town with less and less tourists and students- I assure you - it was quite an undertaking. Bills with absurd figures could undermine the good intentions even with the most stable entrepreneur. And with all this, add the inspections of the government which, instead of ensuring the legality to those who do business honestly, only has a capitalistic mentality.

"Dr. Versace, but we must do something after all." Nothing: this sentence had zero effect on me. Wow, it's strange not to feel anger, disappointment, despair! Even now, when I think back to that moment, I remember the feeling that went through me. You know that feeling when a big burden falls off your shoulders? Yes exactly. It was as if I had suddenly gained a burden that did not grant me happiness.

Inside of me I already imagined, and celebrated freedom. Energy that would have made me chase what was, from there on, what I had always dreamed.

"Wow, I'm exactly where I am supposed to be. This fine is opening my eyes. This is my reality!"

A turning point, a moment of revelation, of light. Like all those important moments of life where you see, hear and feel clearly where to go.

The health board fine wakes me up again. It's like a shot of adrenaline and justice that pushes you to move forward, where on the other side arms and legs are trying to hold you back, attempting to stop you.

It is like when you have been driving for hours in the fog. Holding on to the steering wheel, with your head tensed pointing forward and you are trying to see the road. But you don't see anything. Only for a little while, then, suddenly, the sun comes out. The fog disappears and everything is clear again: the perfect perspective. You notice what point on the road you are on and where you want to go. Tension disappears, the muscles relax, the back lets go of any effort. You stop being stiff and you stretch on the car seat. Even the forehead is less strained and the smile is coming back, together with the breath that regains freedom. That evening and that fine had this very same effect on me.

A snap. I leave the bench of uncertainties, doubts, and hesitations. The focus of my life stops being fogged and gains back clarity. I become aware of what I do not want. I don't want to live in a country where being an entrepreneur is a profession to be ashamed of. I don't want the government to treat me like an impostor, and I do not want to struggle to assert myself, fight every day against out of place check-ups. It is not fair: why do I have to deal with an economy that doesn't facilitate business? Why do I have to get the short end of the deal? I want to be fulfilled as a business owner, I want to make myself valuable, and I want to promise a wonderful future to my family. But we need a country that will 'make it', not a limping country that relies on the hardships of its people. I want to actively do the work as an entrepreneur. It is a courageous profession, challenging and rich of satisfaction. "Stefano, you deserve to get what you want." I gave myself permission to seek happiness. And from that moment on I started believing it, immensely, although never too much. I went home, to my wife. It was one o' clock in the morning and she was waiting for me at the door. I believe those are the people most valuable to us: those who wait for us, those who believe, "no matter what" - those who know to stay when someone else would have already left. She was anxious to know how the visit with the health board went. I could read it on her face. I like reading facial expressions of the people I love: it comes natural to me, without much effort. And it is something from which I am not capable of escaping. Carolina, my wife, knew about the health board visit. Our coworker Ivana had warned us about it earlier today. And she was there, waiting for me at the door. In silence, with that sensitivity that makes her stand out from the rest: she knows the power of words and knows how to use them. She caresses me with her glance and welcomes me, knowing already what I am about to tell her. There was nothing good to come from those inspections. I smile at her while I take her by the hand. "How did it go?" she asks.

"Very well, you know? I have understood everything. Do not worry because as of tomorrow we are going to work on changing our lives, and getting out of here."

That evening the real adventure began. If someone had asked me before what point my life would have taken a turn, I would have never imagined it would have happened that way. We are conditioned to think that change requires endless projections. They instill that in us from childhood: impulsivity is frowned upon. Yet, that evening, I didn't think at all. And looking back now, the times I was overthinking things, got me stuck, instead of leading me in the right direction.

The beauty of awareness is that it hits you like a lightning bolt on a blue sky. You don't expect it, you don't plan it, you don't project it: you simply feel it because it is happening inside of you.

All you need is an image, an unusual emotion, a random gesture, and it rises up inside of you. Straight and direct, like a shiver that aims from the heart to the head. And it is exactly when you least expect it that your life changes. Every change requires a new goal and each new goal embraces a new life- aligning it to the rhythm that you give it, to listen together with your loved ones. That would have been our new goal:

"To make a wonderful symphony out of our life" (Leadership Seminar – Roberto Re).

The embers had already caught on fire. The spark was there. We were lit up, alive. Nothing would have been the same. Not even us.

EUPHORIA: THAT ENTHUSIASM THAT FILLS YOUR SOUL

The following day I woke up in a new world, everything had changed. Even the order of priorities seemed to be askew. Everything that appeared in the previous twenty four hours (as important as they might have seemed), magically lost all impact on me. Other aspects, on the other hand, which I had been ignoring, suddenly began to develop on their own.
I got up charged, light, and full of new energy. I had yet to know what I wanted to accomplish but I knew that I wanted to immediately start. Now my dream cannot wait any longer. I am frantic, sometimes confused, because of all this potential energy. Not a very common feeling for me at that time. I feel that enthusiasm move around and inside of me, like an unstoppable wave that wants to be ridden. "Nothing Stefano, you have entered the first phase of change" – I would answer to myself now, if the 'me' of today could have talked to the 'me' of yesterday.
I made my entrance into the dimension of euphoria.

When you feel your life changing, there is a force that moves you and protects you from everything. Suddenly you are so determined to bet that you will make it. It does not matter who is against you, it does not matter what will happen: you will be successful. Suddenly you feel almighty, without an explanation. And everything seems so easy, and that euphoria becomes a state of productive intoxication.

You start to think, talk, and act as if you are invincible. After reaching a new clarity of prospective, you shift into gear. You go from first gear to the third, then from third to fifth. And from fifth to the eight, because when you're so euphoric you are already ahead of everyone.

Sometimes you go so fast that you don't even notice the difficulties that you encounter on your way. Indeed, you do not even consider the possibility that there will be obstacles, setbacks, or unexpected events to stop you. You are positive: inspired inside, inspiring outside. You make phone calls, take down information, and construct a business plan. Day after day, you take the project of your own life into your own hands. Then you reread it, take it apart, correct the strategies, because deep down you know it: the more you modify a project the more you strengthen it. It was the first stage of the project, to decide what, where, and when and even more importantly, with what resources. Four questions; simple but powerful. When you ask yourself a question, you have to pause for a minute. Not all decisions are taken while moving. And it's exactly here when euphoria has its first hesitation: when you realize that change is a sacrifice and that sacrifices are not easy to handle. So you need to look at one thing at the time, and recess the adrenaline.

I started to ask myself the first question.

What to do? This idea had been on my mind for a while. But it's like it happens with food blenders, if you don't press 'pause', you can't see what's inside. I stop, and Carlo comes to mind, the guy from Vicenza I met in Caracas, during the five years I spent in Venezuela. Carlo managed a few gelato shops there, for the past four years. The most attractive aspect of his job, apart from the economic stability, was the large amount of time he had available.

"To be master of your own time, Stefano! Think of how nice it would be to have your life at your disposal." The more I thought about it, the more I wanted something like that. I wanted a job like this. Imagine what it is like to work and have control of your time. No strict schedules to respect, no time cards to stamp, and regardless of how much you earn, the temporary autonomy will make you feel rich and free as you are.

After remembering Carlo, my memories returned to Urbino. On the same street of our restaurant, my wife and I became friends with Walter, Franca, and their daughter Roberta. They were also owners of a gelato shop, and in the past we had tried to collaborate by opening a new shop in Perugia (but nothing came of it). Nevertheless, I often fantasized with them to leave Italy and start a gelato shop abroad.

These two memories started to outline my dream. The idea of the product to focus on was there. At that point we were not indecisive anymore about what to do.

There are knots that untie in a chain reaction. A little bit like the domino effect. After bringing to light of 'what to do', also the 'when' appeared easily: as soon as possible. The one point that was still a bit vague was where to open the gelato shop. No doubt, it would have been a place where we would love to call home.

You can't think of your job as if it is a separate life: while you are working, you are living. And you can't live in a place and in a way that doesn't belong to you.

Before Urbino we lived in Caracas, Venezuela. The climate there was optimal. Think about it, 12 months of summer during the year! The socio-political and economic problems though, did not and would have not played in our favor. South America did not have conditions to guarantee the stability we needed. "Let's choose a place that has a similar climate", we told each other. Therefore a welcoming place, with warmth that would have made us grateful every day for choosing it.

The matter of the location is a very important at this point of change. We were going to inaugurate our third intercontinental move in the past 7 years. Our older son, Alejandro, being only 6 years old, would have to learn his third language, and this time, without the advantage of having a parent who spoke that language perfectly. We did not pick a temporary country. "This time we can't make a mistake".

We studied the market of gelato. To marry quality of life and potentiality of market is essential when you want to put down new roots. After a bit of research, we decided that the United States would be our ideal place to start our new adventure. The reasoning was simple and logical. First point: we wanted a place that offered us more guarantees than the fragile reality of South America. Second point: we wanted the numbers of the market. And in the United States there were only 900 artisanal gelato shops versus the 36000 concentrated in Italy. To conclude, third point: we wanted a welcoming and warm environment where to start over and feel home again.

Florida won. In particular, Miami: the dream of many, the reality of few and for us, our next life.

ACCEPT THE DIFFICULTIES IN ORDER TO CHANGE THEM

We answered the first three questions. Now it was the time of the fourth question mark, which, as you can imagine, was a little more complex. Now that we knew what to do, how, where and when, there was one knot to undo- but with what resources?
We were in high seas. To open a gelato shop we knew that we needed at least 150,000 dollars. In reality, we found out later, almost double was needed. "Let's not make ourselves illusions: we'll have barely $20000 selling everything we have." We wanted to be honest with ourselves. To look at and accept reality doesn't mean that we have to succumb to it. Instead of what one could say, this is a fundamental condition for change.

We cannot change what we don't see. Only by accepting reality we acquire the power of transforming it.

The decision was taken and we couldn't allow an economic hurdle to stop us. Or worse, to decide for us. It can happen that you believe in a project but don't have the resources to make it a reality. However, this reality could be changed: it was enough to make someone fall in love with your own dream, someone that had the resources to invest in it and the desire to believe in it.

Stage two had started: the one with the difficulties, the 'step by stop' where we are often tempted to stop it all. It is typical for any respectable adventure: at one point the complications arrive. In our case, we are talking about expected complications. Even before we entered our dream we knew that we didn't have the necessary resources and that the difficulties would have been quite many. But we also really wanted to believe in it.

There, to desire something is like having magic powers. Without realizing it, you are surrounded by the best allies: optimism, realism, and exasperation. In this precise order.

We knew that we didn't have all the resources but we were optimistic about being able to obtain a good part of it by selling the restaurant.
"With sacrifices and creativity we will reach two-thirds of the sum we need." We say. And then, as with all the young couples with children, we trust in the help of my parents. But on both fronts we are soon disappointed. On one hand, the Italian economic situation fueled the resilience of investing in an inflected sector such as the restaurant business. Finding someone willing to get into this in a short time was not easy at all. No one seemed interested in spending the sum we asked for and we mostly found people who wanted to rent the business.
We then begin to tour all the bars, restaurants, and clothing shops in the province of Pesaro. We are exasperated but we do not give up. We offer the venue to over forty Chinese families and more than sixty real estate agencies. But nothing, nothing to do.

Three times we almost reached an agreement with three potential buyers. All three times, at the time of signing, they pulled back.

Ok then – time to re-evaluate the restaurant. After all the sacrifices, we have to play it down. "It was a bitter pill to swallow. We would have to reshape 90% of the economic potential we rely on. And the hopes that we put into a positive leap of our future were low at this point.

"But if we really want to change this is the way. What's more important for us? What we leave behind or what is in front of us? " The desire for a change had remained intact despite the difficulties. On the other hand, "there is always the option of asking my parents," I tell myself. So I talk to my dad. I am laying out the project, replying to all his doubts and answering his questions. Like a tennis match, I do not miss a beat.

After a series of objections he announced his verdict. Dry, cold, pronounced in lapidary tone. "Stefano, I will attend the performance of your failure as a non-paying spectator." To paraphrase a song by Massimo Ranieri, my father's words became stones that hit me and my dreams while flying. I'm shocked, without words, on the ground, with the pain as those who are hit by a rock while flying. And not only: who threw that stone was not just anybody. He was my father; one of the people I trusted most. That was the last time I heard from him before I contacted him several years later. And it was also the first of two times when my dreams were wavering.

DETERMINATION AS AN OPENING KEY

After that phone call, my dreams were shattered. Just like me. But it is exactly when you are broken in pieces that you are ready to enter the third phase of change. The phase where you are tested before your dreams come true. The one where you ask yourself, "but how much do I really want this?"

It's a test of life: if you want to fulfill your dream, it's not enough to just believe in it: you have to prove that you deserve it.

That same day I tell Carolina that the 'parent door' is closed. Indefinitely. And that we don't have any other doors to knock on. The next two hours were funny, thinking back on it. After days of running around, researching and going in a frenzy, we were now in the room staring at the walls, in silence.
"We thought and tried all the roads possible since that night on the health board visit. Two months have passed. And yet we are not ready for what we planned. "
It was clear to both of us that we could not have improvised our future. I felt disoriented. What did I miss? Which gear is missing to start the motor? What features does this dream need to have? Then I suddenly remembered a class I attended when I was an insurance agent. "One of the characteristics of a goal is to have an expiration date." Here is what was missing! A deadline within which to reach the goal. No excuses, no delays.
"We have to give it a deadline: otherwise it's more

of a whim than a project." The next day I called my trusted travel agent in Caracas.

"Lina, please, let me know if you find a date with the cheapest tickets available for Ancona-Miami ?" She checks: "July 24, 2013." I do not even think about it for a second in fear of thinking about it too much. To stop at the last minute before jumping, to change my mind because of fear of change. "Book the tickets."

I hang up the phone. My heart beats tremendously as if it was going to jump out of my chest. I sit down. I can't believe it! I did it. I seriously did it. I did like someone who points everything he has on a single number of the roulette. I'm a fool. We already had little money but now I spent most of it on four plane tickets. And who knew at that point if we were actually getting on that plane! At that point I had news to communicate.

"We are leaving on July 24th!" Carolina opens her eyes, smiles at me. Takes a few steps toward me. Then, a bigger smile. "So we have two months to find the funds. We should start today then, right? "She was serene, serious, and wise. She had just received news in a logical way completely out of ordinary logic. My wife and I have always been in perfect harmony: she is the first person to whom I am grateful for every day. Her trust gave me power. Certainties, trembles. Yes, we would have done it.

"We will make it. We'll find the funds one way or another. "

THE DESTINY OF A DREAM IS YOUR JOB

A dream's destiny lies between difficulties and the determination. The first ones are unavoidable: no use of taking on a project without anticipating challenges. Problems, unforeseen circumstances, and obstacles are included in the package.

The secret of the successful person is the ability to not stop in front of obstacles.

The maker of a dream is the one who transforms the limits into new beginnings, issues into opportunities, and unanswered questions into new creative ideas. In every difficulty, an opportunity is found. And how you approach things makes all the difference.
How many times do you see a limit like a problem? That's why it becomes a blocking factor. The cause of the limit is usually considered external, rather than internal. Then the "blame game" begins: whose fault is it and who should be blamed for what? In this distribution of blame, it rarely happens to make yourself part of the list.

When a project is successful you take the glory, but when it fails, it is difficult to recognize your own responsibilities.

Life puts you in front of obstacles to see how you are prepared to overcome them.
By now, we were given expiration date, which for me was already a goal (not a limit). I knew by that date the problems that prevented me from fulfilling the

dream would have to be solved. "Stefano, do your homework," I said to myself.

A homework list always helps to come to a quicker solution. I highlight the two aspects on which to focus: to analyze the whole project and find the capital funds to invest in start-up. I could not afford to have missing details catch me by surprise, once I took the flight.

I turn to my Italian friend in Caracas, who has always been a valuable counselor. He sends me back to the leading company in the semi-finished gelato and confectionery industry. The factory is less than half an hour from my home.

"Hello, I'm Stefano Versace and I'm going to go to the United States to create the largest chain of artisan gelateria."

I introduce myself at the meeting with Giammaria, commercial manager and son of the owner. Listening to such words anyone would imagine they are in front of a professional gelato artisan (or, at least, a capitalist ready to invest in an expanding industry-Or, the more, someone who combines both skills).

Giammaria is silent. Then, with his accent from Emilia Romagna, he asks me how long I've been using their products.

"No, look. I do not even know how to make gelato!"

I do not know what I would have given to keep a picture of his expression at that moment – a mix of disbelief and loss.

"Are you investing in overseas capital?", he gives me another chance.

With the same confidence as the previous answer, I repeat: "No, no. In truth, I do not have any money. "

At that point, I think Giammaria thought: "Look if I, business manager of a million-dollar enterprise, do have time to waste on someone like this."

But his curiosity and playful nature got to him so much, he asked me what my idea is to become the leader of a sector that I not only not know but in which I do not even have a penny to invest.

"I have a plan!" And I begin to explain it. I tell him that for the part of the know-how I would rely on them, and specifically on a gelato course that they offered in a few days.

"For the financial investment, on the other hand, I'm looking for a partner on the site cercosocio.it (lookingforinvestors.it)". He holds back a laugh. You can see that he is starting to like me. He calls a newly hired salesman of the company who specializes in the States area, Michele. With Michele I'm exchanging ideas and information, the same ones that I already tried to get in the previous days by calling Italian gelato shops in Miami. I also tell him about Antonio, a gelato artisan from Caserta, that I found during my calls: he started the same project that I'm thinking about in Miami Beach, and in a short time he has become one of the best around.

I compared all the data I had with Michele. The goal was to build a solid, realistic and structured business plan. He followed me with patience; he was supportive; a little because it was his job, and a little because the request came from the owner's son. And a little because, as he himself told me, he saw "the fire of determination" in my eyes. The one of whom knows exactly where he wants to go.

They introduced me to Luca, their US manager. From

Genova, soccer fan of the same team, Sampdoria, full of positive energy and very competent. Immediately a connection was born between us.

QUALITY QUESTIONS FOR A LIFE OF QUALITY

The first task had started and it was time to go to the second. I had to look for the funds needed for the investment. Michele introduces me to a guy from Elba, also intending to open an gelato shop in Florida. In fact it's easier to find a 50% associate partner than a shareholder! Michele and I immediately agree on things: same values, same ideas and project.

The second task also seemed to have been accomplished. Until Michele pulled out, ten days before our departure, because of his father's bad health- another cold shower. We had just put the dream in our suitcase. My wife had already committed to arranging the relocation; we had already sold the car. And in our head - needless to say - we had already landed in Florida. In short, we were already there.

The news of Michele's leaving was overwhelming: the cards had been rewritten and just before the game started, unexplainably but inevitably the scenario had changed, again. We also discovered that we had to get a visa to stay in the States for at least 6 months, and we only had 2 weeks left in Italy. The first availability for a consulate appointment was about a month from now.

No business partner, no visa: nothing was in place. Except for our ideas, which became even clearer now. Anger and disappointment turned into our fuel, the engine that pushes us to look for the solution: the way out of the problem and the way to launch our dream. "We're going to Miami."

One of the things I learned from life is that you have to be careful about how we talk to ourselves.

Our brain has no sense of humor: it does not understand exaggerations, it does not consider the power of words. It just transpires the message. Fearful questions generate fearful answers. Angry questions lead to violent responses. And bad questions can only produce poor answers. You will understand that giving poor replies when you have a project to launch is not helpful. On the contrary...
You have to point at quality questions. Quality inquiries correspond to quality responses and quality responses are the basis of a quality life. Our brain is a trusted hound: it follows the indications given. Direction and intentionality are fundamental variables. Let's imagine throwing a stick to a dog and having him chase it. If we throw the stick into a creek or in the middle of the water, the dog will run in that direction. If we aim at the park or other safe areas, there will be no risk. Likewise, when asked a question, our mind will track it by trying to find a response as quickly as possible and on the same wavelength.
If we ask "why can't I make ends meet," the immediate response will be "because you are poor". And this answer will not help us improve the financial situation by even one penny.
So, good and positive questions have to be asked.

The right question would be, "What can I do to earn more?" At this point, our brain no longer answers "because you are poor". You are no longer asking it to identify the cause, but the solution. You are facing it with a goal and no longer a problem.

We never stop falling into the pitfalls of the mind. What is important is, to notice it and when it happens, not to lose balance by stumbling upon your own fears.

One bad news after another, my brain was also tempted by the old 'comfortable' habits.

"Why does it all happen to me?", "Why is it that I'm wrong every time?", "Why is there not anything that goes in the right direction?"

So I stopped, I took a breath. I got back in touch with myself, and I told myself:" Stefano, what can you do now to start again finding a business partner? Ask the question pointing toward a solution and you will get an answer that will come to the solution."

So I went back on my computer and to my dream. I started to browse on cercosocio.it again. About 700 checked profiles and about 40 selected contacts that seemed trustworthy. I called all of them, and selecting the calls, I was left with about 12 people to meet. Of those, only 7 got to know me. I stop by Mantova in a café, in Genova in a pizzeria. I even end up meeting one guy in a waiting room at the train station.

And then I meet him, Nazzareno, a satellite technician from San Benedetto.

We meet on the highway exit of Pesaro. He is around 50: white hair, married with two kids, tired of Italy and a dream of a new life in America in his pocket. I show him my project.

"I'll think about it, I'm considering another option for London. But I'll let you know." That was his answer. And he held his word. As far as, ten days later, he was looking for me to give me his decision: we could get to the facts and start with the project. Finally, the doors for the States were opening for me. We had all the relevant information, the know-how learned at the practical and theoretical level, the support of the leading company in the market, the contacts with the two leading suppliers for gelato machines, the financial and associate partner. The pieces of the puzzle were coming together and seemed to fit easily. A few pending details were still missing. Like the visa for example. Yes, the visa. I get in touch with the US consulate in Milan and with an excuse of urgency I get an appointment for the Thursday before our Tuesday departure. We go to the consulate and my wife, Nazzareno, and I obtain our visas.

Second detail to be solved: Urbino's restaurant. I had to find someone to trust with its management since we had not been able to sell it. Meanwhile, time is running out and we do not know what to do. We cannot close the business because a closed restaurant is invisible. The only alternative is to choose who to give it to. We try with some street restaurant owners, friends and acquaintances, but nothing. Nobody seemed to want to take this burden. Then on a Saturday morning as I set up the tables at the restaurant for lunch, a guy walks in, clean face, about twenty years old, Neapolitan accent and much desire to get in the game.

"Excuse me, do you by chance have a job opening?" he asks me. I look him in the eyes, stay in silence for a

few seconds. I listen to my inner voice and tell him:"
Come in, sit down. So what's your name?"
And his answer: "Vincenzo". I'm still observing him.
He is shy and a bit embarrassed. I don't want to mis-
place him, but I feel it's worth the try.
"Vincenzo, do you feel you could handle managing
this restaurant?"
He looks at me wide-eyed, empty mouthed. He
doesn't know what to say, he didn't expect this.
He tells me about his understandable doubts.
"Imagine the scene. I come in to ask for a job as a
waiter. Expecting the typical 'No, thank you, we are
not hiring". But instead…"
"But instead", I continue, "you are in front of a fool
who tells you, 'I hire you' but also 'I give you the
keys of the restaurant and you can manage it all by
yourself". I knew that, in fact, mine was a gamble.
I was placing my restaurant in the hands of a perfect stranger and I wasn't even going to be around to
check on him. But the alternative would have been
to shut it down and that would have been worse,
surely. Maybe, in the end, leaving the restaurant to a
young, inexperienced stranger was the lesser of the
madness we were experiencing.
And then Vincenzo embodied perfectly a philosophy
I've always believed in:
"If someone offers you an opportunity but you are
not sure that you can do it, always answer yes.
Then you learn how to do it." (Richard Branson)
In two days I taught the guy everything I could have
possibly taught him and he learns everything he
could learn in this short amount of time.
Monday morning I go to the bank to sign for a small

loan to support my dream, and the next day we are at the airport in Falconara. It didn't seem true: we could finally relax and enjoy this long awaited and imagined flight. Our life in Italy was coming to an end while this was the inauguration to a new life, looking for the American Dream. We knew that the challenges had just started but, in spite of everything, we decided to enjoy this flight.

After 4 months of anxiety, running around, challenges and endless research, these would have been the first hours of serenity, peace and relaxation.

The plane takes off. "I wonder if, without giving myself a deadline, I would have been able to make it."

I thank myself for having bought these tickets. "Good job Stefano, good gamble." Clearly, this was a winning move.

Think about how often we postpone something that we want to do, with the excuse, "oh well, there is time.", Or "it's not the right time, there will be a better time." This goes for the big and the small goals. Have you ever told a friend, for example, "sooner or later I'll come visit you', and you still haven't gone? A dream can not materialize if you don't give it an expiration date. This timeframe in which you make the project happen is the time from which to start: it's the starting point from where your dream comes true and takes shape.

Successful people give themselves a limit and limiting time is one of the skills of successful people. To give a dream vivacity and coloring it's like painting on a white canvas: do what you want but within the limits and respecting the proportions. How could you, on the contrary, paint on a never-ending canvas? The absence of the limit wouldn't allow you to outline what to represent nor to maintain correct proportions, in absence to any reference. It's like when you decide to start a diet. If you don't have the date in which to reach your goal of losing so many pounds, every time you will see that you haven't made it, you will postpone your results to another day.

The limit is the border for your start, it's the obstacle to test you. Have confidence in yourself and give yourself an expiration date: you can do it. And that will only be the first step of a long journey that you have deserved to walk on.

CHAPTER 2. TO TRUST YOURSELF

Think positive and believe in yourself:
this way you will learn to dream

A flavor for you: Ferrero Rocher
Properties: the softness of hazelnut cream hidden in a waffle. A mix of sweetness and energy to taste layer by layer

HERE IS WHERE YOU ARE SUPPOSED TO BE

There is one thing I remember vividly of our arrival in Miami – it was the humid air as soon as we got out of the airport. I immediately recognized that South American climate. And its climate conditions, that type of Latin energy that Cubans, Venezuelans, Colombians and Argentinians carry with them and deep down, who is around them. Spanish language prevailed everywhere. There were signs, posted on shop doors, saying "We speak English": as if the foreign language around there was more English than Spanish.

And we, having the Spanish language inside us, immediately felt welcomed, in a lovely way. Not traumatic, at least not at that moment.

When you arrive in a new continent, and in particular, a place where you have never been, when you recognize your surroundings at first sight it makes you feel 'less of a stranger in someone else's home." As if the locals told you: "Hey you, you are new around here, but these surroundings already are a little bit part of you."

The arrival in the new continent was exciting and less alienating than we could have thought. The enthusiasm of the landing wasn't traumatic at all. On the contrary, it was as if I had the confirmation of being thrown at the exact location I am supposed to currently reside.

"Stefano, you are there, you have arrived where you were supposed to be. Now we are starting. It's a new start, again."

Truthfully, we had already started months before and the change had already begun.

Now we had to get into the second phase of the dream. The part where, after lots of preparations and preliminary actions, you realize that this so desired and planned adventure, can really start. The planning and simulating times were gone: now we were serious.

REMEMBER WHERE YOU WANT TO ARRIVE

We rent two rooms (one for us and the other for Nazzareno) in the cheapest hotel in the area, close to the airport. Really, it was almost like sleeping on the runway track, where the Palmetto meets the 826. It's a neuralgic know of local traffic. A bit like the junction of Bologna, so you know.

But our finances did not allow us to spend more and so we made do with what we had.

"Don't despise the low because you are aiming high, Stefano. Look at where you are and remember where you want to get." Sometimes all you need is to repeat the goal to yourself.

When the first impact of your change is not "wow", you

have to find a new path, you have to move with intelligence and be content for what you have, in order to reach your dream.

And we needed low cost accommodations. To waste energy by complaining would have not helped. And so we decided to be content with the hotel, just as it was.

These days, when we happen to pass by that Days Inn, on the highway, we stay silent. We smile, and our eyes meet. We look up to the windows of the second story, those behind the palm trees, and then we have a smile on our faces. That smile of who remembers with joy that it was exactly from there, from that room, that the Miami adventure has started.

The next morning we go to Miami Beach to open the company and bank accounts at the Bank of America (I've always dreamed of having a credit card with the BoA logo). As soon as we leave the lawyer's office, where we founded our company, we get the welcome from Miami Beach. Elevators closed due to fire drills, so we take the stairs. It seemed like a metaphor of our lives: step after step, without luxuries. We had to go through every 'floor', we couldn't afford to skip a step, or to be too fast during this change. When a change is taking place you have to go through it gradually. Be thorough and think about every step you take.

I start descending the first of 16 flights of stairs and suddenly miss a step. In short, I stumble down. At the time I weighed 238 pounds: my ankle doesn't hold the weight and twists. In a few minutes I'm left with a watermelon on my foot! My first instinct was to weep, to pity myself. To bang my head against the wall with the typical question of a victim who is defeated: "Why is everything happening to me?" I remember that the brain doesn't have a sense of humor. "Shut up and get through it, it's just a sprain."

I don't lose faith and immediately think about what I can do to avoid spending important days in bed. I go to the first CVS (it's a chain of American pharmacies) and buy the necessary kit to walk, even if slowly and in a lot of pain. Bits of gauze, menthol balm, and off I go. Three weeks went by with me limping, and two months after without running. It is what it is.

When life tests you it does it well.

So the only solution is to stay where you are and try to learn as much as you can from this hurdle. Every obstacle teaches us something and those who make us stumble are the best teachers.

BE THE TRAINER OF YOUR OWN SELF

As far as I was concerned, before me were weeks and weeks of walking all over, to find a decent location where our project could take off. "Stefano, you wanted the bike? It cost you lots of sacrifices? Now start pedaling!" Training is the sport of success but you have to be the trainer of yourself.

As long as you wait for someone to come and encourage you, to tell you exactly how to do it, you will make double the effort to see clearly and you will pedal half way. Any obstacle arising between you and your dream is an opportunity to train in order to reach it more efficiently.

Obstacles are placed according to their own logic. You will never find an insurmountable challenge in front of you, unless you can overcome it. Faith in yourself is the real push that brings you to make that leap. When you not only believe that you can but also that you have to make it, you are becoming the phenomenon yourself. And on the other side of the obstacle there is an amazing prize waiting for you. In fact, you start putting on a show. Sometimes you surprise yourself. Like when you tell yourself, looking back: "But did I really do all this?" So be it, there will be obstacles and a dose of harsh reality.

It's exactly with that hard side that we crashed. I'm not just talking about my ankle: that incident was the symbolic inauguration of what was before us. I'm talking about the credit history aspect. Since we were newcomers and inexperienced of how things worked, we thought that having a past as working people would have been enough to serve us as warranty. I mean, it was clear that we were serious! How can you have your own restaurant, for example, and run it, if you have no idea and practical sense of what you are doing? For us our dedication was clear.

Basically, that day I learned the real sense of the word credit history. Credit history meaning a record where all your data as a debtor is recorded: how you pay your credit cards, your phone bill, your bank loans, the payments for your washer or television, your house note, the car note. And it doesn't end here. Because then this data is matched with the seniority of your credit cards, with the number of credit lines and the capacity of payment. The results are summarized in one number: the credit score. The higher your credit score, the higher the chance that the banks will give you credit. And the lower the interest rate that you have to pay.

The credit score is a warranty for you, for the company, and for others. Like a sort of system that recommends itself based on its experience. Even home owners or property owners check this credit score, to decide if giving you their spaces for rent or not. It was clear now for us that our credit score would be a zero.

The first problems arose right away, as soon as we decided to rent a home. They even asked us a year of rent deposit. And we weren't able to invest the little money we had in rent deposits. Same goes with the lease for rental property. We find a place on Washington Avenue and offer $1000 more monthly than what they ask, just to get the place. But nothing, the answer was 'no' and 'we prefer to rent it to someone who offers us $2000 less than you but who has a higher credit score'.

If experience is a teacher, these experiences taught us that it would have not been easy to have our business take off. We didn't have to assemble one piece after the other, but also take the right pieces, those we needed. We hadn't expected to find this wall in front of us, but we were ready to deal with it.

"IT EITHER GOES WELL OR IT GOES WELL" THINK POSITIVE

The problem with the credit score had to be dealt with according to their rules. As far as warranty and taxation, the States did not let anything slide. Within three weeks we found a house, exactly the day before the deadline of enrollment for our son's school (we needed an address to give). And it's a little villa, perfect 'Miami middle class' style, for $2600/month. We deposit 3 months rent. Now all left is the issue of finding a commercial property.

This wasn't a spur of the moment decision, although time was pressing. Yes we had to rent a space, but it also had to be a good space to welcome a plethora of customers. The decision of where to set up a business is a delicate act that needs detail, calculations and incredible amount of energy.

The choice ultimately fell on Miami International Mall: one of the malls of Miami, next to the airport. I look at the layout of the mall and I'm immediately impressed: there were more than 140 shops with of varying quality. There was even a shop specializing in aquatic gym for surfers! In short, there was plenty of room for imagination. Every year the mall had about 12 million customers.

12 million! One does not need a mathematical mind to understand that we would potentially have a million customers a month, if we decided on that space.

I drive to the mall and find a vacant space, in between Victoria Secret, a Clarks shoe store and a beauty salon. Across from there is a Disney store and Gap.

"Stefano" – I thought – "it's perfect. This is where you need to start."

To ensure the space and to have piece of mind I leave a deposit of $50,000.

"It either goes well or it goes well, Stefano" – I tell myself. "You either bet everything on it, or your dream is not worth anything."

And so it goes: $50,000 taken off the budget of the gelateria and put there, as a warranty.

The issue of the credit score didn't get resolved in a 'creative' way: at least not directly. When you enter a new system you have to submit to the rules of that system: you can't integrate and expand in something without being part of it completely. And the rule was: if you don't have the credit score, we want a bigger warranty in cash.

Ok then; to them the money, to me the dream.

IMAGINE YOUR DREAM AND EXPERIENCE IT

I immediately thought about how to get part of that money back indirectly, by saving on other things. Our budget was limited and we needed money for other expenses. I started with cutting the expenses of the architect.
"Stefano, you imagined the gelateria? So now design it."
And so I designed the gelateria, without any additional costs. It's not enough to believe in what you do: you also have to imagine how to best do it, and then actually do it. Experience it yourself.
You can't achieve something that you haven't already seen in your mind. When I say that I am a visionary, I'm talking about this.
Every dream needs a vision. It's like a painting where the colors are everywhere, even in the corners. You have to color every detail and have a clear intention in every brush stroke.
Especially, before you act on it, you have to put your head to it, and even more, your heart.
I knew how our gelateria should have looked like. Now I just had to design it and give it shape on paper.
Another way to get back the $50,000 indirectly was to re-use what we already had. I planned the least amount of construction: I tried to buy used machines and display cases and to adapt to the little resources that we had available.
I put my hand on bang and chisel and replace the yellow and blue tiles from the old store with beautiful white ones. Those that I had already imagined some time ago.
I had to put trust into myself and into the project.
To believe is the essential lever in important beginnings such as this one.

While the space was being restructured I started thinking (or better yet, I started rethinking in a more detailed way) about the brand and the uniform. And then there were various bases to prepare and dozens of original flavors to experiment with before they could be sold.

As the gelateria Versace took form and shape, it didn't go unobserved from the outside. On the contrary: it was in the center of curious looks of the nearby vendors and of its future customers.

Emotion was rising inside of me: the change was happening, and the right levers had been activated, and I had all the support from my family. It was as if, in the middle of problems, nothing could stop me.

The eve before opening day I took off the plastic film and protective structure off the shop: it was as if a curtain was opening! I felt like the show is about to start. I felt like applauding to myself, for all the sacrifices made. Emotion mixed with energy, and that energy turns into a feeling of being moved.

"Stefano, you are ready."

THE BALANCE OF ACCOUNTS BETWEEN DREAMS AND REALITY

The first day arrived: the day where you have to balance the results with reality, with your dreams, with what you have done. The day where you have to cash out the results: good or bad.

I thought about it often, while I was taking the gelato class in Rimini, while I was on the plane, while I was looking for a space in Miami, while I was taking off the yellow tiles of the wall. I often thought about how the first day could go.

Now it was here, in front of me. The beginning of Gelateria Versace & Gourmet was at the door. I will never forget it.

I remember the emotions of people who were curious to discover us. The children crowded over the display case, leaning on it to get a better view. And the adults who were acting composed, calling their children back, when even they (you could see it!) wanted to lean over the case to look at our flavors.

We open the cash register ready to roll. Inside we had $133: that's all I had left in cash. I knew it, but I believe in the power of change of the first day. My bank account was at zero and the credit cards were maxed out: I didn't even have the money to go out to dinner that night.

I had nothing in my hands, but in my heart I had it all.

I believed so much in this project that I had put all my energy, up to this point, into it. Emotions, time, money. I played each move like a visionary fool who dared to deal with reality in order to restructure it and to build his own dream.

Obviously I couldn't tell my employees about the economic risk of the first day. They would have had to deal with it if it had gone wrong. But this was my anxiety and in that moment I decided to gamble my bet with the future.

I did not want my staff to take on worries and insecurities that was not directly theirs. We had to be present, all and united, together for the big launch.

"I already worked in another gelateria. We opened up with at least $600 in change", a staff member recalls at one point. Silence for a second. What do you tell her Stefano?

"Don't worry" – I answer. "I also have experience, and $133 is enough."

I can't tell her that this is all I have. Don't mind me, opening up my first gelateria!

She would have thought "my dear, but how are you planning on paying me if things go wrong? And I didn't feel like dealing with that. I didn't want to plant any seed of mistrust, fear or perplexities.

The beginnings must be addressed as if you are a catapult: you have to throw yourself in it, with all the positive energy that you can muster. And encourage anyone who follows you to trust you and to follow your launch.

GO WITH YOUR HEART WHERE THE EYE LOOKS

And so the big change is taking flight.

5 dollars and 34 cents. I still have the receipt of that cone with hazelnut, the first gelato of our American adventure. Inside of that cone there was so much: there was the inauguration of the beginning, there was the first client, there was the flavor to taste; there was the taste of freedom and of success. Since I barely had any cash at the opening, I tried right away to keep track of the first earnings. Cone after cone, when we exceeded the 40th, I stopped counting. And I didn't believe it, I knew that I deserved it but I didn't believe it: we already reached the sale of 200 gelati the first day! When closing time comes, I tell myself: "Stefano, are you ready to count your first earnings?" I press the button of the totals, and it seems almost impossible, extraordinary. It was as if I had dreamed it. The earnings

were there and they were a lot: this was the answer that I was on the right path.

You should always go with your heart where the eye looks.

$1200 earned on the first day. "Stefano, you made it!".
When they ask me today "how important was it to believe in yourself?" I remember the vision that I had even before I started: I had to make it and I did.
I made the future that was waiting for me, and out of principle I convinced myself that it would not have been any different.
In the phases of a project, sometimes you ask yourself: "Will it go well?" My answer has always been: "Stefano, either yes or yes."

It's not enough to ask yourself a positive question: you have to also give yourself a positive answer.

Negative answers feed doubts and encourage the dark sides of a project.
Obviously every project has its flaws and its weak points, especially at the beginning. But those are not the parts that deserve attention. To tell yourself that it could also go wrong is to focus on the problems, instead of the success of the dream! And at the end you always go where the eye looks. When you drive, for example, you only need a second. You take your eyes off the road, something else is distracting you, and you are already off road.

When the path is clear, success is sure. When you redirect yourself it means that you trust yourself, and trusting yourself means to think positive.

I mostly had wonderful energies by my side. I am thanking my sons, who see everything with joy and who feed me my smile every time it becomes tired. And I bless children in general, with their authenticity and that enthusiasm that awakens everything.

I still see them walk into the gelateria and watching the tiles, smiling. They were contemplating the colors of the flavors with smiling eyes, and played amongst themselves. It was a revitalizing spectacle to be a witness to such legitimacy.

In particular, I thank love. Without my wife Carolina, without her bursting strength and her energy, I would have not made it. Not this way.

To believe in yourself it is fundamental to have someone who trusts you by your side.

The more important a relationship it, the more it serves as a mirror. It helps you to see the light, it makes sides of you come out clearly that were hard to recognize before. Or that you know but that you don't know how to bring out. To have someone by your side who loves you and supports you , who trusts you and encourages you in the achievement of your dream, is like having a tank full of resources.

On the opposite, if the person with whom you share your life doesn't have any idea of what makes you happy and, most of all doesn't do anything to help you, it's worth changing. It probably will not be the person of your life but this is not the problem. The problem is that when you wake up in a few years and you look back, you will have the regret, or worse, the mourning, of not having done what was in your power to give life to your dream.

Carolina and I are lucky. We always loved each other: we fed and restored our love, together with our children. Our relationship is honest, full and complementary: even our emotions work in a reciprocal way. Every time she has a weak moment I am powerful and vice versa. When it's my turn to be down, she magically returns to top position to take me back and to spur me. We have the same feeling: it's a connection of kindred souls.

We have been, from the start, a war machine, fed by love and the engine in our heart.

To trust oneself means not only to put trust in your own ideas, in your own projects, and your staff, but, and most of all, in your own feeling. Today and yesterday I feel like I can trust myself, and who is beside me. And that first day of opening I had my confirmation of it: change was possible, and we were already there, beautifully and with all our feelings inside.

CHAPTER 3. THE POWER OF CREATIVITY

Pay attention to what you say
and what you say to yourself:
words create your future

A flavor for you: Passion fruit
Properties: aromatic, flagrant, refreshing. If its pulp is not ripe it tastes sour. But when it's ripe it becomes sweet and flavorful.

STOP AND TASTE YOUR EFFORTS

The eve of the opening was the first moment where I was able to sit down together with my family, after we closed the shop. Hugs from my wife, while I had my children near me: I was watching them while they were looking at me. We were looking at each other with emotion in our eyes. And it was as if we didn't need anything else, as if everything in that moment was perfect. We proudly looked at our gelateria.

As if to say: "We really made it", more with our eyes than our words.

It was the first time where we could savor our efforts. There were so many hurdles, bothers and problems since we started to work on our dream, that we didn't have time to stop up to that moment.

What a fight, against time! ...... if you don't make it clear of who is in charge time will put your feet on your head and then he takes your shoes off and makes you run around barefoot: left and right, wherever it wants. With us time wasn't able to have the best of it, even if he tried. The hurry of pressure and of the rhythms that urged us in the last months were nonetheless a constant presence.

Even when we had arrived in Miami, we didn't get a break. We couldn't afford it.

"Go on, continue, do not stop" – my conscience never stopped being a hard and tireless trainer. Between a quibble and an unexpected circumstance, we postponed the opening several times. Four or five... and it was sensational but at the same time exhausting, back breaking, and stressful getting there. To that evening, to that earning: to that satisfaction within reach of that receipt that we photographed, and still today keep possessively.

In the end the first moment of relaxation is the one where you can stop and think, and for us it just arrived. "Relax: we made it! The dream has taken off." Inside those words there was the happiness of having put our dream in motion, there was the joy of success, the pride of never having given up. And the anger of who went against everything that hadn't worked in his life anymore and, despite all, in the end, had made it.

DON'T LET DOWN YOUR GUARD AND KEEP YOUR DREAM HIGH

Who gets a good start is already half way there, they say. Truth is, who gets a good start carries with him all the weight of responsibility: the one of fulfilling a huge operation. To make a reality of his own dream: concrete, mature, and fruitful. I have always seen my project with clarity, and that first day, those $1200 earned, I started to taste the harvest. But it's not enough to see the first results to say that you made it. You did the first step, you are on the first stair of ascension towards your dream, leaving off everything that kept you away from it.

Now you can look up and continue, look inside yourself and remain still in your intention. Then, you can look into the eyes of who loves you and is still there with you reminding you to believe in yourself.

One never stops working and holding on. The future is a far away dot if you look at it from the eyes of the present. To transform it into a horizon and in a larger sphere, one that feeds your energy and the one of your team, you have to look at it with new eyes. With the eyes of who is standing in the present with one foot, and with the other, on the next step he wants to take on.

Every time I made another step I told myself: "Stefano, you made it. Now look at your next step, because it's not finished here. On the contrary: your adventure has just started."

To stop at the first finish line is for losers: it's the typical attitude of who binges a result as if he had to stock up of a just earned success, in the expectation that the next success could not arrive or be late.

Every big dream goes through big obstacles before it reaches big goals.

That's why no real entrepreneur gives up, that's why you can't let negative factors bring you down; much less individuals who pollute the company.

Constructive attention is the constant that you have by reminding you who you are and where you want to arrive, while you visualize yourself in the future you imagined, with care and energy. And you talk to yourself in the right way. You need to pay attention to the words we tell ourselves, how we treat ourselves and the value of our dream.

What you realize is the projection of what you think of yourself: how you see yourself and you cope with reality.

Not just the reality that is in front of you – then you risk practicality and concreteness – but also the one coming. I'm referring to a future reality that the eyes of others don't see and are not able to see, if not through you. So then imagination and creative spirit come into action.

BROADEN YOUR PERSPECTIVE AND IMAGINE YOUR FUTURE

To create a successful future you have to, first of all, imagine it. Nobody has a more practical spirit of who practices the art of imagination. Just as no power is more effective than the art of create and give life to ideas. If you have that power, you can even start from nothing and you will transform the rotten reality into a fertile and creative soil for your dreams.

I've always been a visionary and at the same time, an entrepreneur.

Imagination and the entrepreneurial spirit are two things that you have in your blood, but if you don't know how to cultivate them, they will not grow.

This is the winning combination to the lock: until you put in action business plans but can't look beyond that, you won't be able to get beyond.

There is a dimension of the future where the only people who are able to access it, are those you can imagine it. I already imagined it. Clearly, you cannot 'see' everything. You can get a glimpse of the finish line, sharpen the prospective of your mission, and depict the first wrong points of a project before it's even put in place.

To see also serves to foresee, but there are difficulties that are not imaginable.

Some are little things – just like my forgetting about the health inspection – that can escape you and that you risk of finding again just behind the corner. Others you don't even consider: you don't calculate them because you are busy projecting steps and critical junctions that are bigger.

At the beginning it happened, for example, that I forgot the cost of the architect that should have designed the layout of the gelateria. I totally hadn't considered it! I just included the expense of the engineer, responsible for the technical design to present to the city, in the business plan. Obviously a part of my mind had already been activated thinking about saving money, without telling my conscious part. Reality was, I stood there without a budget for hiring an architect.

Where imagination can't reach or stops, creativity happens.

Creativity is the capacity of coming up with alternative solutions to problems that you hadn't imagined and to turn over a critical issue relying on your visionary abilities.

"If nobody else can do it, you will do this design, Stefano" – I told myself while I reactivated my energetic and determined approach. The one I take on every time things don't go as they should go. I thought of it myself, choosing creativity.

So I designed the gelateria based on three styles: white, wood and steel.

This was the design, first and foremost, of all our gelaterie Versace.

Creativity brings you to take extraordinary actions that, if everything went according to plans, you would have never had the chance of discover that you are able to do it.

FACE DIFFICULTIES WITH CREATIVITY

You have to talk to your creativity the right way: it is not a fan of panic, of discomfort, or of negative thinking. Usually the higher the value of what you are risking to lose, the more creativity breaks into a crisis situation throwing itself back into an alternative development. Make it or break it, to tell you in a practical way, especially when you get one of those unforeseen circumstances that you have to get over.

We were in our first three months of opening, when a Saturday – obviously a main day for sales – the power went off in a quarter of the whole mall. The area affected was – obviously – our gelateria. Imagine now that it means for a gelateria to be without power for even just 15 minutes. A 'normal' shop would temporarily interrupt its activities: the shoe store next to us turned on independent lights and was fine during the black-out.

But when you have frozen food or – as in our case- gelato,

the absence of electricity can make you lose potential income in short time. 40 minutes of refrigerated inactivity is enough to make a gelato turn into liquid.

I could have been overcome by discomfort but that way of talking to myself and to treat my future – in this case impending – was not mine anymore.

"Stefano you either do something or solve the problem or you do something and solve the problem".

I hadn't given myself an alternative to failure, and it is when you exclude failure, that you are already on the thinking line of success.

Two minutes of productive panic – it helps, it helps: adrenaline helps – and here I am again. I was in the game again. I started thinking creatively, at the speed of light.

"I don't know when the power will come back. I can't base my future on these next few hours on an event that is neither certain, or real. Most importantly, I can't control it: I am not the one deciding when the power will come back on."

I realized that I couldn't solve the technical problem, but that I could create an alternative solution to this hurdle.

I ran to Sears, a distribution chain here in the US, which was next to the gelateria. I quickly bought a few colored flashlights to illuminate the display case and the shop, while waiting. In addition, I bought some dry ice. I had never seen it in my life, and I was about to grab it the wrong way, risking my hand to get stuck to it. I then placed it underneath the display case of the gelato to prolong its resistance.

We placed the lights around the case which displayed an almost disco ambiance which seemed to have been concocted on purpose to make the mall stand out in the dark.

Moral of the story: while other shops in the area closed

down because of the power issue, that day my shop stayed open. With lots of optical and colored effects that highlighted it. And – easy to imagine – we made a record of sales.
Between the difficulty of the unexpected and the creation of an alternative solution, I made very little time go by.
Not because I had decided it, but simply, because there wasn't time to think.

The higher the critical issue, the more creativity is summoned, to intervene with the magic of who not only jumps over the hurdle, but flies over it directly.

USE THE CREATIVE POWER OF WORDS

To create doesn't only mean to give life to ideas and put them into practice. You can create emotions between one person and another one, for example. I'm talking about that energy that is commonly called empathy.

A way to create a feeling is to use the power of words, most of all during critical moments when you risk a conflict with someone else.

It's us who give power to the words that we consider more coherent to our values and our way of being: we can decide if we want to use them in a manipulative role or an emotional one.
I have always chosen the second one, and that decision, authentic and honest, rewarded me again this time. The challenge arrived shortly after the opening. In short, I forgot to do some obligatory check ups in the shop.

It is known, that there are burocratic details and legal passages that when you think in the grand scheme, you could miss. Especially when you're dealing with the rules of a new country, where, as soon as you touch the ground and barely get familiar with it, you already have to deal with a new 'technical' way of managing your business. We didn't know all the laws. We had just arrived, and we were already harassed by time and productivity pressure that pushed us to start our war machine in the shortest amount of time possible.

We grafted the movement with a minimal economic fuel but with an enormous desire to fight and win.

But the territory, the one our war machine was getting around, was still unknown to us. As much as you can inform yourself, ask opinions of someone already there, go to the business consultant or the lawyer, there is a part merely real which you have to deal with. And in a short amount of time you can't do everything. But what you have left to see – and what you haven't noticed yet – you can only experiment at your own cost, play, courage; risk, success and danger.
So that day the health inspector arrived. Just like that, unexpectedly. The fact is, the guy suddenly stands in front of me. I didn't know what to say, or what the encounter would bring.

I'm sure there is something that I missed, but I don't know yet what it is.

Because – in every world or business – you always find the wheel that is off track.

I got up some courage and met the inspector. In a few moments I realized that for the city of Miami I opened the gelato shop illegally.

It was simple, but unfortunately, irrefutable. I didn't do it on purpose, it was an oversight that I didn't even think about. How could I have hidden something I didn't even know its existence? I admitted that, for an involuntary oversight, I didn't go through a health inspection before opening the shop.

Now: if you forget something in the United States, they won't make you notice it in a polite way.

The law is the law: it doesn't paddle against the entrepreneurial success, but it makes sure it checks that you do everything by the books. And if you don't, it lets you know.

When that day the health inspector presented himself before me, he had an obvious threatening manner. Avoiding eyes and that annoyed tone who looks at you as if thinking: "Come on, now don't come telling me that you didn't think that a health inspection was necessary".

No, I didn't think of it. Or better: I didn't have the time! I was so focused on how to make my first move, or on how to launch the gelateria, on how to give this huge machine fuel, that only I – together with my wife and business partners – saw in its wonderful potential. I was so busy transferring fire, energy and the right vision to everyone around me, which something surely had to fall through the cracks.

And obviously, when you miss a piece, it's never just a small piece. It's always a joint piece.

One of those pieces that if it's missing you risk that the whole structure collapsing, but until you notice it, you go straight ahead to build what you have in mind. I didn't have excuses or justifications.

"Stefano, you forgot a joint piece. Now, you either pay the consequences, or you explain to these people that you didn't do it on purpose and that this structure that you are building needs their understanding to be able to stand up."

Humility, perseverance, conviction. If you don't have these three traits in your eyes, you can't pretend to have anything good from others – especially who is coming to fight a legit mistake on your part.

I explained with humility what happened.

Sincerity of words is disclosed by how one looks at you. There is everything in a look: the right words direct what the eyes communicate to the heart of someone else.

INVOLVE OTHERS IN YOUR SUCCESS

I told the inspector how much the shop had cost me so far. To call my dream just my 'shop' seemed to make it small and stick it in my pocket.

It wasn't a simple shop: it was so much more. It was the hub of my future. Inside of it were the tears shed for the pressure of a world which is on top of you, the anger of someone saying 'this is the last straw", the energy of a dreamer, the reason of who knows how to do business and expects the most of himself.

The gelateria cost us many sacrifices: economical, physical, mental, psychological.

Now it had come to life for us. We literally ripped energy off each other to feed our dream! It was obvious that we would have never risked in such a foolish way to have it taken away from us, for a missed inspection. In short, I wanted to make him understand that we would have never done it on purpose. To be on the sly would have never benefited us: we weren't in Italy anymore!

I told the inspector also of my family, I made him understand that I wasn't going to risk everything on my own, but that I was carrying the load – wonderful, important – of life of who I loved.

For a detail – surely fundamental – and an administrative oversight – that I shouldn't have made – we risked to make it all fall apart. It wasn't just me and my family who would have been left literally 'in the middle of the street', but my employees would have lost their job. The inspector recognized my sincerity, he felt my story as if it was his own and showed me an admirable humanity. The one of someone who knows that things should be done in a certain way but that, not always, have the same motive for when that doesn't happen.

Not always are rules avoided to escape rules: sometimes you skip them because there are bigger obstacles on your own path that are taking all the rest of the energy, the effort and attention.

I was able to involve him with my story, real and empathic, that I built not to justify myself but to show who I really was. In his head he knew his role very well, but in his heart he felt like he was taking part in our imminent fate. Not a judge, not an inspector: even he stepped up a step.

The step of who knows what is right and he does it by unifying justice and personal values.

In that very moment the inspector became the direct maker of our dream: an integrated part of a bigger project that was worth much more of the 'punishment' because a rule wasn't observed.
Our gelateria would have been successful and it would have also been thanks to him, who, instead of endorsing a situation 'not completely legal', would have helped us by meeting us in the middle and fixing it.

CREATE SOLUTIONS STARTING FROM WHAT YOU DON'T HAVE

When I tell this story, I always emphasize how his human approach and his choice of 'overseeing' a mistake were not ways of "promote illegality". On the contrary, they mean everything else.
He didn't give us a fine, and allowed us to correct the mistake and to make up for a situation that wasn't legal. He didn't 'close an eye': he left open a door for us. Instead closing up and become rigid in a moment that was critical for the growth of the gelateria, he was brought to open up and soften.

It's clear now, how the words we tell ourselves and to others, can be defining, create empathy and make the difference in the realization of our dreams.

I could have acted like a macho, I could have justified myself without putting my heart in it, or worse, to go against the inspector to attack him and belittle our mistake. But it wouldn't have been honest for me and, in the end; I would have had opposition in front of me. An enemy instead of an ally and a collaborative person.

When a problem is in front of you can decide if to make it more complicated, or resolve it in a creative way. The true solutions are not found: they are created with what is missing.

The creative has a solving genius inside of him and a successful entrepreneur knows how to combine creativity and concreteness. To stay with your feet on the ground and take long and confident steps you have to look forward: beyond, more, out of the norm. When you are concrete you can already visualize the results that you'll get. As far as seeing those first instead of the problems that are in front of you.

What you see first motivates you and modifies you.

So, if you are someone who focuses immediately on the problems and doesn't look at the goal, you will focus on the obstacles instead of the finish lines. But if you dare look beyond and lean to see where nobody has reached, that obstacle in your head is already surpassed.

To uncheck a problem in your mind is equivalent to already create a solution at 50%.

The rest is sacrifice, determination, perseverance.

LIVE YOUR DREAM UNTIL THE END AND RELIVE IT IN YOUR MEMORIES

When I tell the story of what my family and I have gone through before creating all this, I feel like walking by the cliffs of the journey again. My heart fills with joy but it's like it jumps: it's the confirmation of the emotion and of the draining energy of who has lived their dream until the end.

Sometimes I play a 'game' that moves me. I call my wife and we go over our story together. Maybe we do it after an important passage of our life: as soon as we get over another problem, or after something that seemed heavier than a wall on our shoulders. We have quite a few occasions to run through our past but some of them move us more.

I like to remember the novel written by Dario Celli, in his blog Aria Fritta. We had just started a project and he was already passionate about it. As much as, before the interview, he went to do an online search about me and my restaurant in Urbino. He also acquired pictures of the new shop, of the maintenance work and even of the first receipt that I posted: the receipt of the first hazelnut cone that I will always keep in my mind.

What Dario did, was to put together pieces, to reconstruct our history.

"Stefano, why are you surprised? It's your story, don't you already know it?" – someone could tell me.

I'm reassuring you though, to reread my story, put together and organized, it's a whole other emotion.

Each of us knows their own path and knows how many sacrifices he has done and is doing to achieve in life.

But when you find your story in front of you, with pictures that bring back memories and the words you heard and remembered as if it was a specific moment, the effect of going back in time is reinforced and emotionally amplified.

When we live memories, we are moved. Maybe it's because when you live life frantically you don't have time to notice every step that you have taken to get where you are now. Then you reread the important stages, while you stop a moment in a present, which, back then, was the future that you imagined for you and your family.

To look back makes us see everything again: the changes at work, the 9 moves – 3 of them intercontinental – made in 7 years, the houses, the sold cars, your wonderful children who came into the world, the opened restaurants, the launched businesses, the successes, the failures, and then, that hurricane of anger and energy that swept away everything that wasn't working and launched you to Miami.

And while you realize and go over your past, your feet are touching the same land in which your dream put down roots and is growing.

ACTIVATE THE "GENIUS" INSIDE OF YOU AND GO BEYOND THE BORDERLINE

As far as we are concerned, ours became a reality and is getting better every day, is perfecting, and is correcting to test us for a level of a bigger future.

Today I have all the serenity to enjoy time.
Time is the most precious thing we have.

We have to realize how to make it more productive in order to be able to profit from it: not just in economical terms, but also in time-space general terms. Today I'm able to be with my family, because I have created a system of automatic wealth. I supervise, I'm always operational and alert on economic dynamics, but I know that my physical presence is not required everywhere and for everything.
The creative power of imagination allowed me to make a reality of this. My only economical and financial skills would have not been enough.

You need some genius, as in that pinch of madness, to look beyond the border.

What separates dreams from reality, successes from failures, courage from fear. When you are able to see this line, then, you can unite the two parts: finally you know where you are, you learn to move and to experiment in the difficulties and in the revenges.
The more you broaden your view, the more your mind is opening, and the heart with it. Then every project develops and feeds itself. Your enthusiasm is the first fuel.

Passion finally matures and is ready to harvest its fruit in a ground where it is not afraid to penetrate.

Have faith: open your eyes, do good, imagine the best. Your future is calling you but first it wants to be seen by you. When you dream at a high level, you play and you also risk a higher level: the one where you have to get involved, launch yourself and believe in it until the end, with passion, energy and constructive detail- Even before you PRESS START.

CHAPTER 4. THE INFLUENCE OF YOUR ENVIRONMENT

Look around: isolate the destructors
and surround yourself
with successful people

A flavor for you: Guanabana
Properties: cancer-fighting, rich in vitamins and proteins. Sweet taste, it brings back a mix of strawberry, pineapple, cinnamon and mango. In the Antilles, its leaves were put underneath a pillow to calm dreams.

LOOK AROUND AND STUDY REALITY

When you have a dream you feel invincible: as if you can make it regardless of all the obstacles that you will encounter out there. You go all out. You try to believe even more in yourself, as much as you can. At a certain point though, you are faced with a fundamental variable for success, or at least, for your success: the environment. The world doesn't revolve around you, you are not the world: the world is out there and is ready to welcome you in one way, but to head butt you in another way.

The world which you face is your environment. The environment is the sum of those factors which condition your life the moment you move in a determined contest and with a certain tendency of soul. In Latin we say *ambiens*, in English *environment*, in French *environment*, in German

Umwelt: in any language we name it, there is a reference in the root of the word "circular motion".

Environment is everything that surrounds you.

Some things will happen to you and you have to face them, others you can choose, others you can project and create them on your own making them become reality. As you do with dreams.

The first step to move in a constructive way in the environment is to look around and ask yourself: "what is surrounding me and who is surrounding me?". To complain of something and not endure it doesn't help to make it more agile or to solve problems! You have to take action, especially when you don't like the environment, when you would like to change air, when there are not many resources left for change.

That's what I did, in Italy, when I had to face a reality that was paddling against the entrepreneurial freedom. I tried to do my best to manage the risk of my projects, like with my restaurant that I had in Urbino. When I saw things were not going as I wanted, and admitted to myself that things couldn't go 'better than this', I started to take action.

If you want to change things, you have to observe them and see them as they are.

You can't change a reality that doesn't work, and you can't move to another more efficient one, until you are not becoming aware of what is in front of you and what things you can better, or be different somewhere else. The influence of the environment in your dream is invertently proportioned to the knowledge that you have of the environment itself. The more you know the environment, the more you learn to move: the more you can be realized.

KNOW, INFORM YOURSELF, EXPERIMENT YOURSELF

To relate with the environment is not an easy mission or something everyone can do: you have to have your armor, find the right strength, evaluate with precision flexibility and sternness. You also have to know – as much as you can predict – on what is about to happen to you. After you look around well, it's time to make the second step.

The key word of the second step is "knowledge". The more knowledge you acquire, the more your power over the environment is growing and the less impact the environment will have on you.

It's not so much that the probability of a certain difficulty will diminish, or happen less often, but rather, your chance of unchecking it, will get bigger. You will be more alert, more informed and therefore, more determined.

Knowledge goes through two channels: information and experience.

Information is everything you gather from the outside, the means to get knowledge are many. From information provided by technology to information you can ask directly to someone with has more competence. From that others tell you, the ones who got a feel of the field where you want to enter, to everything you learned and gathered yourself in your archive of past experience. Every piece of information has to be verified clearly, before declaring it a truth, and it's not only the content you have to verify, but also who gave it to you. Where am I getting this certain piece of information from? How reliable are my sources? Am I sure I will find things as others have time before me?

The other way to get knowledge is experience. When I get in touch with an environment and start to look around, I'm already experimenting with it in my own way. There are actual experiences – the ones I'm living in the present and of whom I have a partial vision – and past experiences. The last ones we remember in a certain own way: for reasons of selective memory or emotional filters, we tend to keep those experiences that 'gave us' more. In negative terms, or in positive ones, when something happens, even an adversity, which teaches us a lot, we absorb what it gave us and we keep well in mind, for future times, what a mistake that we made, took away from us.

Experience is a sum of mistakes and archived teachings. Someone who is afraid to make a mistake can't experiment, just as someone who can't get involved is not able to know the environment.

The principle is the same for the environment in which we already are (that never stay the same and are constantly changing) and – especially – for the new one we want to enter: we have to risk and stop "bandage your head' before breaking it. Often we don't throw ourselves straight into a dream because we are too worried thinking about how to turn around, as soon as something doesn't' go well. A favorable environment becomes successful only when you have the courage to put roots into a place and plant your project there.

DESTROY THE SHIPS AND BURN THE BRIDGES OF YOUR PAST

The environment influences your success but you are also doing your part in it. There are capable minds that know how to make the most out of unfavorable environments and weakened ones that, even if immersed in a privileged environment, produce a tenth of what they would be able to.

The environment is a base of your future but you have to make a move. Before you can move and start doing, you have to put roots in the place you chose to be.

To put roots down doesn't simply mean to plan on staying somewhere for a long time: it means to exclude any chance of turning back and only leaving the chance of succeeding in the own venture. It means to face decisions without going back and eliminating any way of escape: it means to "destroy the ships". The availability of a plan B reduces considerable the chance of success and can prevent us to fight until the end for what we want.

There is an anecdote I like to tell, and it's the venture of Hernan Cortes, who left in 1519 for Mexico with only 508 men and 11 boats. Cortes knew very well that his men were exclusively motivated by thirst for glory and money and that they were "serene" because even if the mission had gone badly, they could have escaped and returned to Cuba. To motivate them, he decided to burn the ships, leaving only two choices, for him and his men: to die there, in a foreign land, or to fight the Aztecs and win. The result? The conquistadores and Cortes, even being in inferior number, succeeded in their endeavor and conquered Mexico!

It meant the same for them as it means to you. In some situations it's necessary to burn the ships, the symbolically represent the way of escape to rely on in case of a failure.

The secondary road, when you have an objective in mind, is more of an escape route than a valid alternative to your own dream.

When you put down roots you become one with the environment and with the project you are taking there: they become your home, your dream, your investment, your possibility, your future. To put down roots in a place you first have to detach yourself from another. I call that "other" the "past". No one can work at his full potential and invest energy in the present if he is still tangled in his affairs and worries of the past.

What is passed has passed, so they say. But sometimes it's us who have to leave the past once and for all and let go of the grip.

We look for redemption – economical, affective, and personal – from a past that hasn't satisfied us, and at the same time, we are not willing to let go from it completely. Why? Because in a corner of our mind we are scared that the future, for which we are working and are investing every possible energy, could be worse than the part of life that we left behind! So often you start a project and you leave a way to go back to your own harbor, in case plans didn't go as they should. On one hand the open harbor is a "secure nest" and a source of apparent security. On the other hand though, it takes away the vision of the present and doesn't allow staying focused on what we desire: the realization of our own dream.

Not having any other choice, on the other hand, is the best condition to gather courage and motivate yourself to realize your own success.

It's what I did with myself from the beginning: I cornered myself. "Stefano, it either goes well or it goes well", I told myself. When I left Italy for Miami I invested everything. On the first day of opening of Gelateria Versace Mall I didn't even have money in my pocket to go eat dinner that same evening.

I played everything: every crumb of my soul, every mental effort, every economical and psycho-physical energy. I burned the ships.

If things that day had gone wrong, I would have sunk with my ship like a real captain. But I immediately created the conditions for which I couldn't have given up. Even if I had wanted to, taken aback from a moment of discomfort or anxiety or hysterical perfectionism, couldn't have retreated.

There is an episode that I usually tell, to make people realize how burning the ships was a determining factor for the realization of my dream. We had just arrived in the States, and were busy searching for a space for our gelato shop. Amongst many places, a perfect place stood out, in

Miami Beach. Rent was $6000; I offered $7000, contrary to the usual procedure that happens here. In the States usually a rent negotiation happens where the one with the lower price cut wins. With a price increase I was sure to have gotten the place, but instead, my expectations were disappointed. The place was given to someone who offered $5400: another confirmation that without a credit history to show, earning trust would have been difficult, if not impossible.

This was the second time where I saw my dream shake. I remember it was a Thursday night and I came home bitter, disappointed, angry and heartbroken.

Money wasn't enough to enter in the world of gelato, and money wouldn't have helped my talent, my determination, my willpower or my spirit of adaption.

To put the classic break on my wheel was a technical detail: no credit history, no dream.

I spent the night thinking, in the room with my wife and children who were sleeping. I looked at them and they gave me strength. Then I listened to all my emotions moving inside of me: I was discouraged. In the silence of the room, I started crying. It was a weep of fatigue, of bitterness, of fear. I was scared: I didn't know where to put my hands to make the future happen that I had projected.

When you have done everything possible and something is not dependent on you anymore, what you need to do is to stop and recharge your energy, in order to come back and move better. You have to continue to believe in it, because there will be a prize of perseverance.

On my part I was lucky to have put myself in the position of '"no return": I didn't have any more economic resources to go back and live in Italy, everything I had was there and I couldn't go back anymore. I burned my ships. It's a piece of advice I give to everyone who wants to come to America, who tells me "I'm coming but I'm not selling my house in Italy", or "I see how it goes there and I'll get a work visa here".

You have to burn bridges with the past if you want to build a better future on the base of a new present.

Who wants to be an entrepreneur and is not willing to burn their ships, is probably abandoning at the first difficulty, returning to more stable land and will never fulfill their dream. On the contrary, who burns ships is forced to deal with difficulties, because he can't go back but only move forward.

And it's when you don't give up and you fight, and you will succeed, inevitably.

As far as me and my first shop, the prize arrived the next day, when I was able to obtain a place for rent that just opened up at the International Mall. This place would have revealed itself even more strategic to the one I wanted to rent before. Life rewards you if you make the right choices and you show steadiness, every day, in chasing your dream.

ISOLATE THE DESTRUCTORS OF YOUR DREAM

They seem like normal people. They have a job, probably a family, friends, and seem satisfied in their lives.

But they also have a huge limitation: they can't stand by you while you fulfill your dream. And not only: they will also try to destroy it or hindrance the success. I call them "destroyers of dreams". Sometimes they act out of envy, other times out of protection, other times again because they are too unhappy with themselves in order to support the happiness of someone else. Fact is, your dream is at risk when it comes into contact with people like that.

The destructor of the dream can be anyone: a work colleague, a stranger, someone you barely met, a relative, a friend, your partner.

A belief that betrays us is to think that who loves us can't paddle against our happiness. That's why we usually only recognize our enemies as antagonists of our dream: we identify them in those who are jealous of us, and from whom we could expect anything. But truth is, the most powerful destructors of dreams are our closest and dearest contacts. It seems like a paradox, I know. How can someone who loves us rage on our dream? But that is usually what happens, most of the time.

Very often they don't even do it on purpose. I don't want to exonerate them: it's that sometimes a destructor of dreams puts the spoke in the wheel and is not aware of it. Or he does it saying "it's for your own good".

A broken dream hurts and any defeat is heavy to digest: true. But nobody should throw away their dream to protect them-selves from the risk of failure.

The person who deserves to reach success is the person who is willing to overcome failure, for what he believes firmly.

One of the ability of dream destroyers is that they are able to take down your self-confidence. They take you down, to say it all. Maybe you approach them to speak about your project, full of enthusiasm and the more you talk about it, and the more you feel your excitement sink. You look at your listener and you realize that his eyes are not shining as you wished they were, by sharing your project. Or you jump up and down from joy and think you are holding the most beautiful dream of the world in your hand, and a destroyer of dreams backbites you with a short question: "So, you think you will be successful with this idea?". Or with a dismissing comment: "You are kidding, I hope!"

Sometimes they are direct and aggressive. They do it more for protection than for not trusting your judgement. Fact is that the effect on you can be devastating. Especially when your strict judge is someone you respect, in a human and professional standpoint.

Then his words bombard your dream and with every criticism there is a dowel that breaks off. That's what happened to me when I talked to my dad about the project Gelaterie Versace. ", I will attend the performance of your failure as a non-paying spectator ": I will never forget his words. We are talking about my dad: a successful man who raised me with attention and noble values and whom – I would have bet on it! – would have never said or done something that would go against my well-being.

The more a destroyer of dreams is a person dear to us, the more potent influence he has on us.

Let's think about it for a minute: do we get more offended for a negative comment told by a stranger or by a friend? The power of the words also depends by who is saying them. When a destroyer of dreams is someone close to us, it will get complicated to separate the rational sphere from the emotional. Let's overlap the affectionate dimension to the professional one: "someone who loves us would never tell us anything wrong', we tell ourselves. Someone can have our good in mind, can love us, and be an excellent professional in the field. But this doesn't imply that he knows about our future, or that he is an oracle.

There are no truth holders but only commentators. There are valid opinions and useless ones, but we are always talking about opinions.

If we interpret in this light the contributions coming from the other, any point of view is more an opinion to consider (or to throw out) and an appealable judgement with which to deal with!
At times the destroyers of dreams are strong in appearance but emotionally fragile. I call them fake confidents. It's those people who diffuse a dream and tell you with menacing tone: "I don't want to be harsh, but I'm doing it for your own good." Or more: "Someone will have to open your eyes. Luckily I'm here!". To protect myself from failure – and for a subconscious and selfish fear of theirs to have to bear that someone they love is failing! – they foretell it to you even before you arrive. There are cases where they resort to victimhood just to be able to convince you to give up on your dream. Let's think, for example, to those partners who put the family before your desires, when you present them your idea of jump-

ing into a new project. "And if it doesn't go well, have you thought about what will become of us? Don't you worry about our children and the possible consequences?". The risk you run when you have to do with partners of this kind, is to covers your wings and stay in your secure harbor – which makes you unhappy – instead of evolving into something better, opening up to uncertainty, but also to happiness.

I have been lucky to have my wife by my side that always supported and encouraged me, without making me feel guilty. She was there and I felt her presence: when things didn't go right, she was by my side with her anxiety but kept it to herself. She never weighed on me; she never wanted to burden me: but she was willing to share my burden to make it less heavy for me and the go on together easily.

When you have the advantage to be loved by someone who believes in you and nourishes your dream, you know you can draw double energy from your relationship.

We can accept that a destroyer of dreams can be a colleague, a friend, a parent. But I always advise against keeping a partner who, even involuntarily, can't be happy for us or feed our enthusiasm.

Once we have gotten past a destroyer of dreams of that time, we can confront all the others with a minor influence. Like the free lancers who we meet along our journey, the coworkers, friends of friends, and who judges without knowing us.

After I got over the confrontation with my father, for example, I was able to easily uncheck all the other destroyers of dreams with whom I had to deal with.

Once you recognize them, you know how to deal with them. Or better, avoid them: the destroyers of dreams have to be isolated.

Before leaving for Miami, I climbed over a series of destroyers of minor dreams. The merchants on our street where I had the restaurant in Urbino started to talk bad, when they heard the news of my departure.

"He will make a hole in the water, he will come back with his tail between the legs, without a penny and worse than now", they said. Obviously not to me, but behind my back.

Then there was who tried to destroy my dream face to face. Like some merchants, lawyers, entrepreneurs and experts in the field, who not even tried to fake enthusiasm: "What are you going to do in America? They only eat ice cream there", was one of the less negative comments. I went beyond, with ease: beyond the badmouthing of the envious merchants and beyond the criticism who opened their mouth, without contributing to my dream in a constructive way.

Some destroyers of dreams don't reveal themselves for who they are right away, and only after, once you 'defeated' them, you find out what their real participation is all along.

I remember when I applied for the rent location at the International Mall. Right then I hadn't known their "destructive" intentions and it was something I found out from a third party only afterwards. The owners of the place were aiming to put me into difficulty the moment of the negotiations, in order to make me refuse and stop me from continuing the business. Initially they asked me a deposit of $6,000 that then rose up to $18,000, and then to $36,000. After I accepted that last sum, they rose to $49,000. I thought it was absurd, as if, every time I accepted, they wanted to test me. And indeed, that is what came out afterwards. The peak came when I said yes to the $49,000 – at that point I was driven like a train! – and, at that point, they responded nonchalantly that it would be best to make it an even number. The deposit went from $6,000 to $50,000: I told them with an imperative tone that this would have been the last crossbar that I would have jumped. I jumped it and this was the last obstacle before opening the Gelateria Versace.

DON'T BE AFRAID TO CHANGE

Don't be afraid to change: city, job, friendships, people who gravitate around you. The real change, the one that goes through success, goes through small changes. Start with cleaning up from negative people who gravitate around you.

To take a distance from poisons, your life doesn't mean to remain bitter nor does it mean to be "too hard": it means to respect yourself and your projects.

There is a macro-environment and a micro-environment. We are not responsible of the first one: it is represented by the contest in which we grew up – that, willingly or unwillingly has influenced us – and from the one in which we are right now (and from which we can leave, planning our future projects with detail and thoroughness). The second one is, on the other hand is consisting of the people who surround us and it's built like Dante's circles:

each of us has more "circles" of contacts that gravitate around him. The people who are in the circle closest to you are those who are conditioning you the most. There is a saying: "Tell me who you are going with and I will tell you who you are". Indeed, it works more or less like that. Who you associate with, who is in the most intimate relationships with you, conditions you: with their way of thinking, of doing, of focusing on the values of life, on your way of being and your feelings.

We are responsible of the micro-environment that we built for ourselves: we can modify it at any moment, making cuts or additions, amplifying perspective of view and thought and focusing our beam of action in the working field that we are interested in.

Success is the art of knowing to change with courage, uniting instinct and reason. When you are not happy, you don't have much to lose: you have everything to gain. I met people who, scared of the thought to let loose from the micro-environment that made them happy – and about which they complained every day – ended up staying there in stagnation: tangled between regrets and projects, compromised forever.

There is not an ideal moment for change, and to make perfectionism your own criteria for success would have been deviant and not productive. Every moment is the right one. If you want to change environment (macro or micro), you are already on the way to do it.

SURROUND YOURSELF WITH SUCCESSFUL PEOPLE

When I'm asked what success is for me, I answer that it is the constant and continuous search for happiness. Successful people are not those economically high up, nor those who have family in "Mulino Bianco" and "settled", nor those professionally at the peak.

Successful people are those whose eyes are sparkling: those who never forget to say thank you to themselves, to the ones they love, to life.

A successful person is one who gets up every morning early and does everything to finish the job for which they are responsible. A successful person is a parent who takes care of their children and invests thinking about their happiness. A successful person is who is not letting destroyers of dreams take them down, and fights their own dream. A successful person is someone who went from failure and, challenging change, tried it again, and won. A successful person is one who is happy for other people's success, because they know that everyone is a carrier of happiness in a broader collective.

If you want that success stays in your life for a long time, surround yourself with successful people.

In the end we are mirrors: what is outside reflects in us and we reflect on others what we have inside. To have a positive, authentic, motivated and enthusiastic environment around you gives energy and clears the way for that long awaited happiness.

Any entrepreneur who wants to fulfill their own dream should reckon of how much of himself he is able to transmit to others, and how much he receives from them. To be able to promote synergies with your own coworkers, employees, and in general, harmonize relationships, are essential steps for the success of a dream.

I did it. I surrounded myself with successful people, that first and foremost, I treat like people, and only then as employees, partners, coworkers.

My employees are successful people: professional, motivated, able.

My friends are successful people: authentic, honest, ready to support me.

My wife and children are successful people: every day they give me an immense portion of happiness. They are my fuel, my force. They are – I will never be tired of saying it with pride and emotion – my success.

CHAPTER 5. THE BUSINESS PARTNER ATTRACTION

Let others fall in love with your dream
and trust in the best professionals

A flavor for you: Tiramisu'
Properties: mascarpone, eggs, lady fingers and coffee. The attestation, all to taste, that when you combine the right elements you will obtain a successful result- tasty and satisfying flavor which cheers your mood and energy up.

WHO IS A BUSINESS PARTNER?

Once in a while a new word starts to be popular. It ends up in everybody's hands and in few mouths. As in the case of the word "Business Partner", one of the new professional figures now in style. It's amongst the most complex and researched, so much that a lot of people take on that role. But you have to recognize the most valid ones before understanding how to attract them to you.

Their role consists in contributing to the development of the demand from a client giving them a service – or a product – that is complementing and obviously, effective in the market.

To have a good business partner by your side means to be able to count on someone who is able to analyze the complementarity between his business and yours. And not only: a good business partner suggests tailor-made and integrative solutions to increase the revenue for both.

He has to also be gifted with a remarkable economic mentality: drawing from experience and knowledge, he will then have the ability to customize the own operation relating to your objectives.

He can't be lacking sensitivity: no one can be your business partner if he hasn't picked up the uniqueness of your operation, the investment you are making and the deep value at the base of your business.

In short, a business partner is a high level professional with a high mix of qualities who you know you can trust: problem solving, innovation spirit and respect of tradition, economic foresight, capacity of relations and negotiations, creativity, motivation and, most of all a managerial wisdom and a solid experience of success behind him. Another characteristic that can't be omitted is transparency: how could you share your entrepreneurial project with someone that you don't trust 100%?

Business means "deal", partner means "mate".
A business partner is literally your mate of bargains.

Pick him, therefore, with the same attention that you picked your friends and your partner! He has to match you and, where there is agreement, there has to be complementarity. Remember: winning partner, already "half" the success insured.

CARRY OUT YOUR BUSINESS PLAN

Before you deal with the business partner you have to deal with yourself and your dream. It's a fundamental step: you have to study the numbers of the market and carry out your business plan. Ask yourself what you want to achieve, in what way and with what resources. Because it will be with the answers to these that you will introduce yourself to your business partner for the first time.

In this phase of analysis and projection, the power of numbers will be decisive.

To put numbers on concepts that are not numbers allows to build a realistic and effective business plan. One of the secrets of success is to keep the majority of the data under control in order to project a strategic plan close to reality. That's why, one of the first steps to take, during the making of a business plan, is to insert all the numeric data: from forecast of sales to the distribution of the year, up to general cost (employees, management, raw materials). Up to here, all good, if it wasn't that many neo-entrepreneurs stop at this level of analysis and don't go further!

Success is determined by primarily numeric questions: there are other aspects, or better choices, that modify the results of our earnings.

As the ability to sell your own products and the location of the business in a city over another. Or, the ability to build the right network and that of acquire a circle of co-workers and employees that are motivated and efficient. Those aspects can't be put in numbers, at least in appearance. In fact, they can be converted in numbers, thanks to the power of numberization.

To put something in numbers doesn't mean to numerize – or better, to assign a number to something in order to tidy up – but to be able to convert something in numbers that is not a number.

Numberization is a process of transformation in the real sense of the word: it means to put a number to a concept.

If, for example, you have someone amongst your staff that is a better salesperson than another, your action of putting a number to it will consist in understanding "how much better" the first one is compared to the second one and to assign him, therefore, a coefficient number. The objective is that of being able to approach the value of their sales close to reality. The same is valid for other aspects. Do you have a business that is taken place primarily outside? Through numberization you can determine in what way the weather will affect sales.

Once that you will have understood the importance of number-ization, your business will acquire more effectiveness and will raise your ability of positive reaction to future adverse happen-ings.

You can isolate those sensations and those temporary states of mind that can affect your choices: like moments of euphoria where exaltation can reduce problems, or vice versa, the most crazy moments where you see everything black and infeasible.

Obviously you will not have control over everything but you will be able to foresee the majority of the events that you will put into numbers.

To foresee means to help prevent and get over a critical moment with more lightness and determination. The more concepts you put into numbers, the more you will be realistic, and therefore, effective.

To put numbers into non numbered concepts is a rare step that not many make, but it's an essential step to elaborate a entrepreneurial strategy, almost perfect and impeccable.

BE BRAVE: NOT PERFECTIONIST

It seems like a paradox but I assure you that it's not. To give a shape to your dream you have to let go of the aspiration to perfectionism. On one hand things thought and done in an approximate way don't work and are not a sign of professionalism. On the other side the claim – or worse, the fixation – of programming everything in the most minute detail boils down to standstill and delays the realization of your business.

If you let yourself being transported from the mania of perfectionism you will never make that first step that will inaugurate your dream. To be successful you have to be brave: not perfectionist!

With that same courage you will attract the right business partners: it's the passion for a project – non its mere programmation – to make others be passionate about it. So do your best: accept that some aspects of your dreams will escape control and prepare yourself from now one to face unpredictability.

Don't listen to the limit that others set: try to climb over them as if they were challenges.

Roger Bannister was the first athlete that ran a mile in less than 4 minutes: something that, before his record, was regarded impossible if not at the cost of dying. According to a study by a scientific research at the time, no human heart would have been able to withstand such effort. After him, 300 athletes crossed that limit! It was the proof that the real limit wasn't of medical-scientific nature but exclusively mental: once Bannister proved the fallibility of scientific research , the other athletes followed. Success is contagious, as well as failure.

Keep in mind that bright business partners are lovers of innovation. Innovations associates with uncertainty and it's a bond that a dreamer can't free himself.

To be dreamers means to be visionaries: who dreams sees what nobody has seen yet and takes new roads, not yet taken by anyone. A perfectionist will never be successful: instead of undertaking something innovative and uncertain, he will aim to have the guarantee of the result holding on to something more traditional and less risky.
To attract the right business partner you have to be innovative. And not only: you have to have gotten rid of that cliché' that slows down development of any dream.
Stop saying "your situation is difficult", and to impose the "challenge to help you and fix it" on someone else. A business partner will not solve your problems but will

contribute to the diffusion of your innovative solutions. Stop complaining that what is still missing in your project: react and show yourself proactive.

Isolate yourself from clichés ("everyone says that…", "but I found out that..."): test and experiment reality, exceeding the limits of success that have been imposed by others.

Do as the hornet does. Because of a body mass too heavy for its wings, the hornet would not be able to fly: but it doesn't know it, and that's why it's flying! Challenge your nature as well to discover hidden resources.
The main well of energy to achieve your dream and attract business partners is to believe in it until the very end.

INVOLVE PROFESSIONALS LEADERS OF THE INDUSTRY

"A professional is expensive!". There is another cliché that we have to get out of our head. We have this idea that high ranking professional profiles are the most expensive, unreachable or, if reachable, they come with a high price. When you have your business, finding a partner who collaborates with you and supports your dream is an investment with two hearts – yours and his – for something that will bear fruits for both.

One of the limits when wanting to start your own venture is thinking with a mentality of a dependent.

So you see the business partner as someone "to hire", or, vice versa, like a suitor in front of whom you have to fake to be "beautiful and competent" to attract his attention. Wrong! A business partner is an ally and an important column of your business: with him you have to be yourself.

Looking at reality, we have to admit that nobody is able to do everything in detail.

If you want to be successful let go of the image of a spin doctor: the image of someone who is an expert in every aspect of his project. It's counterproductive.

The more you will draw from the best professionals in X sectors, the more time you will have to dedicate to what you love and know to do. In my case it's to do business strategy: to pull the reins and understand what the next objective is to move toward, motivating staff and business partners.

When you select a business partner, the quality of your selection is fundamental.

The more you will involve the leaders of the industry, the higher the guarantee of your success will be.

When I picked Carpigiani and Mec3 I was very selective and aimed high with the awareness and the determination of who wants to get the best : I wanted to tend the bow and, with the arrow of my dream, hit the people that would have helped me fulfill it. Carpigiani is leading the industry in machines for producing artisanal gelato since the 40s, and innovation is at the base of its technological leadership. Mec3 is the first company in Italy in gelato production and for years it has been operating with its dedication to transparency, authenticity and food safety. Thanks to their contribution, the dream of Gelaterie Versace has been able to take shape and expand at high speed.

When you have an entrepreneurial project in hand, the rule is to think big.

I aimed high. And I got to that high because in my head and in my heart I had nothing but my dream.

YOURS IS A DREAM, NOT A WHIM

Remember that the way you see your dream will depend on how others will see it, particularly a business partner. You can have developed an impeccable business plan, but, if you don't really believe in it inside, your project will never obtain the merit it deserves. Meaning that it will not be successful or, even if it would happen, it would be reduced compared to its potential.

When you introduce yourself to someone that you want to recruit as your partner, you have to be clear that on that chair it's not just you sitting, but also your dream, and the "you" of your future.

Nobody would invest time and money in a project that doesn't give the idea of a future.
The problem is that often, a business partner is sought out not as an business ally, but as a "solver" of problems. The imagine projected is not that of a self-confident entrepreneur, but of someone scraping up help without any capacities of problem solving. At first, if we get rejected,

we don't even realize what image we gave out. If then we don't have the fortune of having someone by our side that gives us a "yanking", we risk spending the future years of our live with the conviction that the others didn't deserve us. Our dream dries up and we reproach our experience to the neo-dreamers, to subconsciously turn off their enthusiasm.

Before you show up to an interview with a potential business partner, ask yourself if you would invest in yourself. And if yes, how much.

To tell yourself how much you are worth in economic terms will help you to enter in a more practical and real dimension. You can't pretend from someone else what you first and foremost don't think of deserving.
Then get rid any probability of failure inside your head: you are about to tell someone that he should invest in your project and your determination cannot be "weakened" by insecurities.

In the end, present your business plan broadly, without dwelling or digressing. But most of all, have fun because in the end you are playing it: your dream is on the line.

Who cannot have fun with a dream, means that he is not taking it seriously enough. When you are close to a project, you want to feed it with positive energy, smiles and authenticity. The smile not only helps to dissolve tension but also to create a line of communication more spontaneous and emotional with the other. To speak in an impeccable way of a project is one thing: to move someone emotionally, while talking about a project is a complete different story. Of success, clearly.

Sometimes you have to meet wrong business partners until you find the right ones.

The secret is to not bring yourself down. Yours is a dream: not a whim. For a dream one is willing to fight even after a rejection, an obstacle, a mistake; for a whim, instead, the field is abandoned at the first difficulty. The alarm goes off when we believe to have a dream and, at the first risk, we are terrified from fear of losing what we are looking at. *"And if I make that choice, then I could lose X things"*, *"If I move, I am risking to throw away my savings"*, *"If I launch myself into the void, I could lessen the quality of my life"*.
But success is hiding inside risk.
You can never reach it if first you didn't go through the "forest" and through your insecurities. When you have a dream you are afraid to lose the chance that is presenting itself in front of you, rather than that bundle of things that you already have but that is not enough to make a person happy.

MAKE OTHERS FALL IN LOVE WITH YOUR DREAM

Imagine having a dream but zero resources to fulfill it. In your mind everything is more or less defined. You see the lever points of the project, those critical and those that can be improved with time. You have a clear and meticulous business plan where you pondered factors of every possible difficulty. You have potential coworkers who, at the start of the project, would be ready to be operational. You have a partner on your side who supports you during the projection of your dream. It's also an extreme trust that this dream could become a reality. When you have the vision of the whole of a project, you look at it in a more ample and evolved way compared to how others can see it.

When you introduce yourself to a potential business partner, he starts studying you to understand who he has in front of him: the first aspects he points his attention at are those "technical" ones, and it is normal that the emotional part is put aside. After having checked that the idea could work, a good business partner should go on to phase B, the so called "reading of the eyes". It is, in reality, a reciprocal test: on one hand he weighs on how much passion and determination are inside of you, on the other hand you can realize if you have a potential clever business partner in front of you (who also considers psychological aspects) or someone vague and professionally meager (if he is not interested in exploring more than your words).

That's what happened between me and Gian Maria Emendatori, the son of the founder of Mec3: after an initial "technical" interview, we immediately became empathic toward each other. My friend from Vicenza, who was in Venezuela, had suggested I go to Mec3. I listened to his enthusiastic speech and , with the same energy, I ended up shaking hands with Gian Maria.

"Hi Gian Maria, I am Stefano Versace. I'm going to the United States to open the biggest chain of gelaterie in the United States."

"Tell me Stefano! Tell me!" – Gian Maria said with a romagnolo accent – "How long have you been using our products?".

"No Giamma', I don't know if you have understood… I don't even know how to make gelato!"

Gian Maria tried to hide his perplexities bouncing back another question with nonchalance, with that friendly romagnolo accent.

"Ah. So you are doing a financial operation?"

"No, I don't have any money."

Gian Maria tried to continue: "So how are you thinking about doing it?"

"With a business partner!"

"Ah, I see!" – His tone was relieved. As in "thank god". And he continued: "And who is he?"

"No, I don't have a business partner!" – I answered with authenticity "I'm looking for one, on cercosocio.it!"

Silence. In fact, thud. For a moment we both thought that the dialogue was ending there. "Gian Maria had the expression of who is asking themselves on how to get back those 5 minutes of his life wasted on a charlatan. I decided that I had to play all my cards. I broke the silence and told Gian Maria of myself, why I had this dream, what moved me, the vital importance why I had to fulfill it.

"Versace, I don't think you will make it" – finally said Gian Maria "But in case you should make it, I could never forgive myself to not have grabbed you when you stopped by here." He called Michele, the responsible for Mec3 Sales in the States, who, by a stroke of fate, had returned to Italy that day.

"Let's sit down". – Continued Gian Maria – "We need to talk more and see how we can work together". In this dimension of faith the alliance with my first business partner flourished. Mec3 fell in love, in a certain sense, with me. In fact, all the symptoms of falling in love where there: I arrived suddenly, I left them without words, I displaced them, and finally, I was welcomed by them in fear of losing me.

This anecdote is a testimony of the importance of transmitting your own passion when you talk to a business partner about your dream.

It's not enough to have a dream: you have to transmit how much it means to you and how much it could mean to who you have in front of you: for them, and for the others.

ACCEPT CHALLENGES AND BUILD YOUR FLAVOR

I've always been a visionary, I've always gone with my mind beyond of what my eyes saw in front of me. To be a visionary has its reasons and makes you responsible of a great and delicate mission: that of fulfilling what was seen.

In my case, it was my dream. When a dream manifests it happens that you don't have all the necessary skills yet. I didn't have any idea of how to make gelato, for example! I did my courses to learn, but the moment I met with Mec3 I didn't even know the basics. The same story repeated itself when I signed up, by invitation of Mec3, to Gelato World Tour, an international competition that has the goal of making gelato known to the world. I was already in the States and the Gelaterie Versace already took shape, when one day Luca Farotto called, manager for Mec3 for the Americas.

"Stefano! I would like that you participate: it's an important event and a challenge, and if you win, you can make the difference for us".

At first I was perplexed. I didn't feel equipped with necessary skills to compete in such an important competition.

"But I know nothing about gelato!" – I answered.

"It's not important. You take part in it, try it and build your flavor".

I think that a business partner needs to be amongst the first people to believe in you, in your capacities and in your project. When someone trust strongly in us he also becomes our motivator. Either in the sentimental field, or in the personal and professional one. To have the fortune of who supports you and pushes you to try is something wonderful.

I liked the idea of building my flavor. I found it not just a personal challenge but also a personalized one: I would have never competed to just present my technical skills, but also my story. I thought of a flavor that would represent me, and my mind wandered into childhood. When I was a little boy I loved ricotta, cannoli, pistachio and candied oranges. I could have not inserted them into the flavor I was about to create.

If you don't get involved with passion, if you don't present what has a sense and a value for you, you will always compete with half of you and your potential.

I called the flavor "Scents of Sicily": the flavor had a scent of that land. I even dared with the choice of the name. "Flavor" seemed trivial to me, almost discounted and limited. Good flavors carry something magical, that brings you back in time and reignite memories and passed senses. The scent immediately sparks a sensory association and it's faster than the taste to awaken memories.

I showed up to the competition: there were sixteen gelato artisans from all the United States and Canada. I won. It was an unexpected victory: I ardently wanted it but never expected to get there. The technical prize as best gelato in North America was awarded to me. I was first in the United States. It was an amazing recognition: with a personal flavor, produced by uniting heart and skills, I won a competition in which, just a few weeks before, I wasn't even going to participate.

After this victory I was sent to the finals in Rimini: it was September of 2014: I returned to Italy and I found myself in front of 24 gelato artisans from all over the world. Obviously there were also Italians, in this round. From there the prize giving, unexpected, amazing.

My gelato received the prize from the public as best gelato in the world, and even more exciting, with a detachment from the second place with over double the votes.

They started to talk about me in the newspapers, interview me, asking me curiously how I succeeded in such a great enterprise. I felt satisfied and grateful: to myself, to my family, to my coworkers, to the public and also Mec3, who encouraged me.

With that phone call a few months before, Luca motivated me and launched me toward a new challenge: that of building my own flavor and expose myself in front of everyone as a gelato expert.

Then in Rimini I met Achille Sassoli, Event Manager for Carpigiani and responsible organizer for the Gelato World Tour. If I wanted to achieve a quality product, I had to not only rely on raw materials of good quality (like Mec3) but also quality machines. I picked Carpigiani as my second business partner. And never had a choice been more precise and timely. I made another step forward toward my dream. I was happy, amazed by my successes and satisfied.

TRUST THE BEST AND RELY ON YOUR OWN

Quality products, raw materials of quality and quality business partner generate a quality business. It's inevitable. When you trust the best, you become better too. A mistake though that we make sometimes, is the one of exceeding the threshold of highest esteem and to slip into from the recognition and reciprocal trust into a sort of "dependence from others' opinion" and the incapacity of autonomous choice.

When you have an ally who plays professionally on your level, you trust him and you hand him – so to say – the "ball" every time there is an obstacle to overcome where you know he will handle it better than you, because that's an obstacle he is specialized in.

To entrust your business partner to make decisions in an industry where he is the leader is a strategic, valid and winning move.

The critical issues arise when you start to trust your business partner more than you trust yourself. Remember: it's good to delegate responsibility keeping in mind each other's skills, but the primary responsibility of success is yours.

Trust the best, but rely on your own. Business partners represent a higher gear, the level to make a jump in quality (to guarantee production, for example, or facilitate distribution, or increase sales): they are not your anchor of rescue!

Always keep that primordial energy with whom you attracted them because it will be that same energy that will keep them tied to you, making them feel like they are an integral part of your project.

When we depend on the professionalism an judgement of someone else, we lose the "centering": we feel insecure, we lose our decision making power, we underrate our capacities and we forget of how much we have done up to this point.

To keep the reins of your dream in hand is fundamental: you are the one driving. So trust yourself, experiment, verify and if necessary, give yourself permission to change your mind. About yourself and about your business partners. Keep in mind that anyone can make mistakes and restructure themselves in a better professional way.

Another important aspect to keep is constructive criticism: always be critical but never polemical.

A critique is the observation of what is wrong: it is necessary to point out the "obstacles" and to reformulate strategies to advance better. If you point out a mistake to someone but don't give him suggestions on how to improve it, you are arguing... not criticizing. A good leader is also a good critic, towards others but also towards himself: he knows how to make the right observations and invites his professional net (business partners included, why not?) to also do the same. The best business partners are those who know to critique when necessary: not those who flatter, neither those who slow you down with sharp and polemical notes.

The more you believe in yourself, the more you will be able to involve the right people and the more your dream will increase in driving frequency. Or better, flying!

CHAPTER 6. THE SEVEN TYPICAL MISTAKES TO AVOID

A flavor for you: Lemon
Properties: Light, fresh and cleansing, rich in vitamin C and anti-acid, it's a simple and delicate flavor that purifies and feeds the soul.

WORRY ABOUT THE QUALITY OF YOUR MISTAKES

It's a typical attitude that one has when talking about the road to success. You are afraid to fail and mistakes terrify you. For some strange reason the mind is lead to focus on the quantity and not the quality of our mistakes.

"How many mistakes did I make? How many will I make? Many? Too many? A few?"

If you want to start your business you have to forget the number of mistakes: most probably in the future and already done in the past. Rather, focus on the quality because it's there, in the "how do you act", the key for change. There are mistakes so small that, adding them up, they will never make the difference. And there are oversights that, on the other hand, risk to block your dream, to slow down the rhythm of advancement. When you worry about the count, you neglect the content!
To shrug off a mistake with carelessness can make you regret, in a second moment, of not having had the right care.

A dream is like a crystal cup: brilliant and delicate. If you know how to handle it, it will not fall on the ground and break. But if you make that abrupt movement that makes it slight off your hands, there, it will shatter. And it will be difficult to restore it.

Up to here I showed you that there is a lot of "know how" to do before launching your own business. In this chapter I will show you the other side of the metal. Specifically, I will tell you of "what not to do" to avoid that a dream gets interrupted, or worse, fails upon the start.

I will introduce you to seven mistakes: simple, common, essential.

Simple because it's easy to fall into it. Common because they are based on general convictions. Essential because it's enough to make one in order to compromise, automatically, the work you have done up to now.

Never underestimate your own capacities, the possible difficulties and the eventual critical issues.

At the same time never underestimate a mistake: some are reversible, others are not. You can learn from all mistakes but after having made a few it's impossible to resume the point where you were interrupted.

"A warned business man is a half saved dream"

Let's analyze together the seven typical mistakes to stay away from if you want to do international business.

DON'T BE ARROGANT: YOU HAVE A LOT TO LEARN

"Americans who come to Italy always compliment us for our pasta. Stefano, I'm almost coming to Miami and will open a pasta shop in the States!"

How many times have I heard a comment like this! At first, every idea seems exceptional, especially when it comes into your head.

We are all genii with words, and on paper every thought is the right one.

Maybe one day you get up, you feel inspired, you see your professional situation in a different perspective and ...voila'! You convince yourself to have discovered the Holy Grail and to be destined in a few moves to become a successful entrepreneur. As if there is nothing left to learn and you already know everything! In fact, we Italians have an excellent education and valid ideas too. But this doesn't make us "the best".

To have a valid idea on paper is not enough to ensure success.

Success is the result of the integration of real competence, right beliefs and effective judgement of the market. The first mistake that one makes is the one of arrogance: to feel "on the top" and perfectly ready to master any challenge, when instead there are other stages to surpass and knowledge to gain. If you really care for your dream, it's essential that you keep your feet on the ground. What to do with a genius idea if you don't have the competence to put it into praxis? How can you root a project into a reality that you don't know almost by heart?

Success goes through knowledge: as much knowledge as you can gain, you will get to a point where it will be sufficient, but never too much.

When you hide in arrogance, you shut yourself down toward reality, and taken by self-love, you put aside what is around you.
You preclude in the discovery and neglect important steps: the evaluation of the environment, the finding of other information, the creation of a professional network. There is always something more that you can learn: in short, it's better to claim knowledge than to assume to already have enough of it.

In the stage of gathering information, you will clearly have to turn to the right people and resources: the key word is reliability.

I could happen, for example, that someone sent you some data that seems unreliable. At that point you have two alternatives: the first one is to assume it is wrong, and throw it out. The second one is to dig deeper and verify, together with the person who sent you the information, the point that don't match. It's the "breakeven point" of knowledge: that in which you learned up to moment X meets-crashes against what you are learning in the moment. X+1, and so you have the chance to "question" your ideas.

To have success nothing is more harmful than the standstill of thought. In the business world, who doesn't change perspective is destined to succumb!

You know Darwin's theory of evolution? The weaker species disappears because it is not able to draw the right sources from reality, while the better one progresses and survives. But who are the best? The best are the strongest: it's the profiles that know how to adapt to the environment to gather little by little, the best of it. To be flexible and dynamic doesn't mean to be opportunistic and fragile minded.

Only the insecure don't feel confident enough to change an idea.

When you change an idea you are improving an idea and make the approach to success and to your business easier. It's not said that what you have done so far is wrong, but surely from this point on you can do better. This stands for anything: every success, from the smallest to the biggest, can be improved. Every objective can evolve in another more assumptive one. Always ask the best from yourself, but do so avoiding presumption and perfectionism.

DON'T IMPROVISE YOUR SUCCESS: PLAN IT

No one is born an entrepreneur , neither does one become one from nothing. You need experience in the specific field and in the industry where you are thinking about starting your business.

Planning is needed: success is not improvised.

To plan it, you first have to reset yourself on the right *modus cogitandi*: are you thinking about your project in a logical and intelligent way or are you getting excited about an idea that is not defined yet?

"This idea will be very successful abroad because it is already working greatly in Italy!"

The second mistake to avoid is to be vague and to combine all ideas in one. Remember that your success is like the amazing leaf of a plant. The more rooted and deep the roots are in the ground, the move resistance will arise to environmental disadvantages and the plant will evolve at its best from its shape. Sometimes an idea, without beginning or end, could also have a "moment of glory", thanks to some luck. But it is a temporary success, almost sudden, that will fade away soon.

To do international business, you have to feed your "plant" with steadiness, thoughts and right rhythms.

To think that a project can be successful overseas as well, just because it worked in Italy, it's saying like you could water a cactus with the same quantity of water than you give an ivy.

"Why would I need to plan the launch of my business overseas as well, if in Italy that project has been tested already?"

When I get asked a question like this I try to make the person who asks me understand that we are talking about two distant countries, and therefore, two different realities.

What you sow in one ground can't root in another.

Therefore you first have to decide what energies to invest and how, study your territory well: inform yourself on which country you would like to go to, dedicate your time to gather the right information and analyze the reality. Laws, regulations, life styles, tastes, customs are characteristics that change according to places, but, when you try to improvise your own business anywhere, they all finish up in the same cauldron and create confusion.

To study the reality can make you realize that you don't know anything yet about certain aspects of your project.

Always show humility and courage, and with intelligence, go over the steps of your journey: you can adapt your business and remodel it based on the training that you have, or maturate the basic proficiencies yourself to supervise your dream.

That's what I did when I had no idea how to make gelato and signed up for training classes.

The binomial on which a winning programming is formed is given from the combination of observation spirit, humility and courage.

Through observations you open yourself to the reality that is around you and you relate yourself to the potential market. Through humility (is it coincidence that humus in Latin means "land"?) you keep your feet on the ground and you get out of an egocentric prospective. In the end, thanks to courage, you launch yourself toward what your observation spirit and your humility suggest.

Courage is nothing else but the wise capacity to act following your heart.

If you want to go overseas, leave Italy behind you, inform yourself on what is waiting for you and create a space in your mind where you can reword a "new world": that of the country which is waiting for you.

UNHOOK YOURSELF FROM THE PAST AND STOP COMPARING

"The lights in Miami last 7 seconds! Those in Italy only 3." It's really true that the human mind is insatiable! It is never satisfied and always finds a reason for which to complain. Complaints are a shortcut to stay exactly on the point of life where you are right now: there, still and stagnant, covered by the alibi to stay "in the wrong conditions" they don't allow you to really be happy.
For the ones who are not able to stop comparing the new country with the old one from which they came from, there will be a nice red light for them.

A "switch" of obligatory mentality if you want to catch the flight.

You have to format your mind according to the right logic: orientate yourself toward problem solving, focus on the objects and explore. As long as you lose time rethinking about how you are better off or not in your old country, you will have less time to invest in the analysis of the new reality that is around you, therefore, in your project.

It's a question of gradual training: every time you want to compare, think of the time you are losing and talking about something that is not relevant for you anymore.

Avoiding to invest your energies in useless thoughts , you will earn time that you can utilize in a more useful and constructive manner. As, for example, the analysis of the new reality where you are about to start your business. Once you start to get to know the first rules of the place, you will start to think in line with its rules. It is important that you don't feel like a stranger, but an integrate part of the country. Familiarize yourself with the customs and interactions of the place: it will help you to improve your marketing and sales strategy. Don't take any information for granted and no news for something sure and established.

There is a physical and philosophical principle that underlines the importance of unhooking from your past: it's the principle of void by Newton. Newton invited to free yourself from what no longer serves you, to create new spaces – voids – where you will receive what is yet to come. The more your mind and life will be clean and "up to date", the more you will live in the present without those weights of your past and you will be open to absorb the beauty of renewal. And the power of success.

Welcome change, leave behind the past and renew yourself.

FIND GOOD PEOPLE AND TRAIN YOURSELF TO DELEGATE

Confidence is on your side until it shows up to paddle against you. And it starts to paddle against you when you keep all the important decisions inside of you, without trusting anyone else: from business partners to coworkers to your staff.

To know how to delegate is a fundamental ability because it allows you to build a net that is working, economically efficient and functional.

Above all, if you want that your projects grows fast and with agility. A successful business feeds also from teamwork: the more you synchronize yourself with your professional contacts, the more you will be able to work in synchronicity with them.

"Yeah, but I don't trust them! If the other one makes a mistake, I will lose out!"

It will have happened to you as well, at least once, to think that. The first step is to surround yourself with good coworkers and in selecting personnel savvy in the field.

"Quality choices will bring quality work."

When you learn to delegate, you don't just motivate your team, who feels appreciated for their efforts, but you also make it easy on yourself. You will notice that, leaving the chance to follow the procedures to each of them, you are saving time.

Time is the most precious resource that you have available.

With time you are able to think, project, build. You can rest, get back your energy, be with the people you love. With time you regenerate, and at the same time, you generate wealth, When I learned how to delegate, I found out how nice it is to do what you are meant to do: in my case it was to do strategy, to amplify the visions of my business and to build international nets. I trust my coworkers blindly, to the point that, sometimes I avoid to say my opinion because I know that each of them have a top knowledge in their field.

A last mention goes to the spirit of redraft, in other words, that flame that stems from inside and reminds you of past times, when you were the employee. Maybe you weren't treated right, maybe you would have loved to be acknowledged. In the new role of an entrepreneur though you have to manage and rework the bitterness of your past.

You don't have anything to prove anymore, if not to yourself. Believe in yourself and you will produce harmony and wealth.

OPEN YOURSELF TO DIALOGUE AND TO THE COLLECTIVE BUSINESS

Another mistake that one sometimes makes, is that of keeping the Italian mentality of "if you think like me, then I have to make you change your mind." At the bottom of this belligerent behavior is the conviction that the others want to harm you and, if they notice something or give us advice, they are criticizing us more than encourage us. Not everyone wastes their time to share wrong considerations with you! Obviously, there will always be someone who will give you a wrong piece of advice. But before you deem it that way, listen to that person. Especially if you think they are professionally or humanly able to do so.

It's essential to open yourself to the dialogue.

In Italy there is a tendency toward crash rather than meeting: we Italians are more worried about saying our opinion rather than listening what others have to say. To stay firm on your idea during an exchange of points of views will not allow you to improve it. Often, it is that way to stay that makes you ponder around the same question, without coming to any constructive agreement with the other person.

In America you are cut out of the business if you don't mature the ability of listening and communicating. Here belligerency is seen negatively, and it is not considered constructive to invest time into talking to someone who is only interested in being right. Substitute belligerency with coherence. That way you will contribute to the collective economic business, which is the real aspect of market value the US points to.

HAVE A SENSE OF MEASURE BUT THINK BIG

It will seem brutal but this book also serves to wake you up. If you want to think small and you haven't left for overseas yet, you still have time to stay home. America is not made for modest dreamers and for who settles for dreams with a small size.

"I want to open the best restaurant in Miami!"

And why not the best 500 restaurants in the United States? An aspect on which to ponder about is the balance between what you give and what you want to obtain in return.

You always have to ask yourself if the dream is worth the sacrifice.
The bigger the sacrifice, the more your dream has to be at its level.

So you not only will feel paid back but also satisfied. What are you leaving behind and toward what objective are you headed? A change of country, language, habits, rules, is an important evolutionary passage. It's a launch toward your dream, in a certain sense, also a jump into the void that involves you and your family. You are uprooted from your "natural habitat", the one you know perfectly even if you are tired of it, to go towards something that you don't know how it will welcome you. Your dream will reward the sacrifice if you think big. The sense of measurement comes before everything!

Measure yourself and adapt your ambitions to the affective, economical and emotional investment that you have made. Dream as you deserve.

Think about multiplying your successes: in the USA it works like that. All the restaurants here, are chains: also the luxury ones. If a business model works, it reproduces itself automatically; if not it stays closed within itself. Are you ready to expand and multiply your dream?
Who has a dream doesn't minimize or belittle it: who has a dream thinks big and, as soon as the first success is gained, repeats his winning formula.

DON'T GIVE YOUR DREAM TO A THIRD PARTY: AVOID FRANCHISING

And here we are at the last mistake. Last but not less important, because as with the others it is important with the success of your project. Once your project has been completed in the first phase, you will have to deal with the collective economy of the States. I'm talking about what I mentioned earlier: you will be called to repeat the formula of your success to expand it.

A mistake that is easy to fall into when you are not an expert yet, is to trust franchising.

In Italy it is called that way because it's the only terminology that we know to refer to a commercial affiliation. It's a type of contract between two subject, economically and juridical independent, where one give the other availability of property or intellectual rights (as brand, commercial denominations, signs, patents, utility models, technical and commercial consulting).

Who generally wants to be affiliated with someone wants to open a new business, but at the same time, doesn't want to start from zero: that's why they prefer an established brand and starts from there.

If you say franchising in America referring to this type of contract, they look at you in a strange way. Here the appropriate term is "licensing": it's a type of franchising that doesn't exist in Italy, to be clear.
When I realized that my business could have been scalable, I started to think of how to open new gelato shops.

The easiest way that I thought of was, in fact, the licensing, since in the US it was a common business practice. I made a genuine mistake, typical of a novice entrepreneur. And to think that I had been warned indirectly, years ago! When I hadn't matured the idea of my dream yet, I was talking to the owner of a huge chain of gelaterie in Italy and Europe. "God forbid! I don't want to hear about it": was his comment, as soon as I mentioned franchising. At first, I didn't understand the reason for his reaction: how come he turned down franchising, especially he who had used it at the beginning of his activity? Just after having committed his same mistake, I understood why.

When you give your dream to someone who is not you, the results will be inevitably different.

Imagine a person who doesn't have your history, your experiences, your upbringing. They probably don't have your values, your objectives, your stimuli and your motivations. They will do things differently than what you would do: not because they are incompetent, but because they are motivated by a different personality. The success of a gelateria is not just the result of a correct business plan and an impeccable business strategy: it depends on many little details and shades that are essential. Clearly, these aspects seem superficial, if not insignificant from someone who looks at it from the outside. However, it is the exact opposite: the control of toppings, the relationship with staff, the production of fresh gelato every morning, the use of quality raw materials, the authenticity of the relationship with the client, all this makes the difference. There could be someone, for example, who wants to save on cost and cuts those 8 dollars of personnel to produce gelato in the morning and prefers to recycle the leftover flavors from the day before.

But it doesn't end here: there is also a creative, emotional aspect.

The showing of flavors in the display in an arranged order, the combination of certain colors to evoke a certain sensation of who is looking at them, the offering of side products (toppings, mini-cookies, water bottles), these are other aspects that add to the rest. Not to speak of the relationship with staff members. My staff knows it: I pay them to sell, not to scoop gelato.

There is an emotional and formative dimension that is at the base of the performing one.

If you don't know what is behind every flavor, if you think that ice-cream and Italian gelato are the same products, if you limit yourself to hand over a cone and look the other way, and not smiling to the person you hand it to, there is not success that will hold over a long period of time.
That's why, after having appealed the licensing, I realized I would have not gone far had I continued. The consulting experts who recently joined the company also gave me the confirmation of that fact: if I hadn't stopped in time, not only had I ruined the name of Gelaterie Versace, but the actual gelaterie wouldn't have had the actual speed of reproduction. I would have crashed against failure.

There was also a complaint from people who had taking my gelaterie in licensing, saying that they had bad luck with them.

It's a typical Italian mentality: if things go well it's their own merit, but if they go wrong it's someone else's fault. There was someone who fought against me because he wasn't able to have the life style he was hoping for, by the failure of his gelateria. Is that surprising? The quality of motivations determines the beliefs and the beliefs are determined by success: it's not enough to manage an already established gelateria to reach it!

When you trust your dream in the hands of others, success will never be the same. Not for you, not for them.

At this point you will have to use a good part of your energies to solve problems of who is complaining, rather than creating something wonderful starting from the last result you just reached. Today the Gelaterie Versace are 100% ours: we don't give them out in leasing to a third person. Through technology and informatics, training courses, detailed data analysis and standardizing of production methods, we were able to keep a direct control on the quality of products and of the work that is behind. I am happy and satisfied. Who fought my project and believed, in a destructive and sick way in my failure, is gone. My dream, on the other hand, has grown: it has strengthened, it has matured and it is even more solid than before. When I say who is not willing to make mistakes will never be successful, I am referring to that criticism. I am grateful for my mistake because it has allowed me to take a step back to run up again: toward wiser decisions and strategically winning ones. And, most of all, toward my dream that is growing, every day more.

CHAPTER 7. AUTOMATIC WEALTH AND THE ECONOMY OF WELLBEING

A taste for you: A taste for you: Pistachio
Properties: Antioxidant, nutritious, antibacterial. Strengthens the eyes and protects the heart. A protein concentrate in a classic, but original, delicious and strong taste.

CREDIT HISTORY AND CREDIT SCORE

These are two typically American concepts, but for an Italian who wants to come to America it is crucial to know them.

I'm talking about credit history and credit score. In the previous chapters I have already told you how I became familiar with them and here I want to explain how they work best.

The first represents the history of your debt. The second is a number that defines the quality of your credit.

Let me explain better: credit here ranges from a minimum of 350 to a maximum of 850 points. If you have a negative credit (usually between the 350 and the 560) it means that you have had economical and financial problems, and hardly anyone will trust you from this aspect. If you exceed 740, you have an excellent credit and others will rely on the morality of your person.

In practice, your credit score is your business card. The catch appears the first time you arrive in America. Because, at the time of your arrival, you have a zero credit score and unprecedented credit history. You can not claim credits / debts from your country of origin, and the only thing you can do is to persuade people to trust you, offering your way of guaranteeing.

As I told you, that's what happened to me when I was looking for a home and a place in Miami. In the end, I had to give $50,000 in warranty, taken to the extreme by the store owners, who were still testing my economic strength by raising the figure from time to time. Those $50,000 are there, still to be collected. On the other hand, however, I have shown not only to have solidity but also economic mentality. Versace gelaterie have multiplied and reproduced the same success in many cities.

My credit is currently in the range of excellence. Last Friday I bought a car and returned to pay for it on Monday. Why wouldn't they think that I would run away with the car? Simple: I have a high credit score and, of course, an interest in not dropping my score (after such a theft the credit score would go down drastically).

Credit moves in positive (grows) or negative (decreases) according to the regularity of your payments. If you meet deadlines and are punctual, your credit score increases.

Linked to the credit score are then the credit lines: in practice they represent when you are trusted by banks. It seems a paradox but it is not. The more lines you have, the more chances you have to be in debt, and the more the banks trust you. The more credit cards you have, the higher your credit score will be.

Every time you pay late, or have problems with accounts (even small amounts like utility bills) or you use your credit line too much (exactly over 30%), your credit goes down. The reason for this: for the American system you can also have many credit lines, but if you go beyond a certain limit of use, you are considered a risk-prone individual, and therefore unstable and dangerous to them.

Credit also goes down whenever banks and financial companies check the level of your credit: the impression that comes up is that you need to be "verified", or you've asked for more loans.

Technically, it is about" inquiry", which means inquiries.

At each check, the score drops two to three points. The more banks see you, the lower your credit score: if you check ten banks over the course of time, you can also lose 30 points, just to be clear!

One last detail is that if you have no debt, you do not have a good credit.

For the US financial system, it is essential to know how you pay your debts before making a loan. You ought to have many debts and pay them well, then you would be a model of the welfare economy. You could become an example of a successful American entrepreneur: a risk-averse but a lenient person who knows he can be indebted but also pay, trustworthy and 100% weighted.

The Italian mentality tends to reduce the risk and think small: in America, on the other hand, the more you are willing to risk, thinking bigger, the more you are worth it, and at that point become a resource for the collective well-being.

THE ECONOMY OF WELLNESS

The first to talk about the welfare economy was the English economist Arthur Pigou in his book *"The Economics of Welfare."* From the academic point of view, this is an economic discipline that studies the reasons and the rules of some social phenomena to formulate solutions that aim at achieving an optimal situation. Removed in reality, the concept of "welfare economy" can be applied to the American economy.

Here, if you really want to do something and be supported while doing it, if you want to accomplish your business and succeed, you have to think big. Or, better, in "collective".

Any business that produces wealth for the person in America is intended to multiply (if it works) or to become extinct (if it does not grow). Your success and your wealth fuel, therefore, overall US productivity. You become part of a system that, once you have achieved credibility, you will find more people open to dialogue and collaborating than people who are ready to raise walls, controversy and fight against you.
The average Italian in America will be called upon to revisit his thinking systems (more closed, rigid and individualistic) to adapt them to a more agile, collective and "expansive" social and economical reality.

You will achieve success alone, but once you've got it, you multiply it and expand it with the system.

It is a system that favors the wealth of those who think big.

Americans define rich people those who have a million dollars in availability and at least half a million dollars of automatic revenue.

I believe that anyone can be "rich" from the start of their business. The rich person is the one who can create automated revenue higher than the chosen lifestyle and gradually increase it. Therefore, do not underestimate the value of your time. Especially if you are in the initial design phase!

Remember that it is from time that everything is generated.

If you arrive in America and have only few entries, worry about getting time back by temporarily adapting your lifestyle to your earnings. You will get paid back later. Invest your energies to mature the right idea: that way it can be sown and collected, to nourish you and the whole collective economy.

WHAT IS THE WEALTH (FOR YOU)?

The word "wealth" is in the mouth of all but one rarely realizes that the concept of wealth should not be generalized, or even less taken for granted. We talk about it often but each one of us conceives it differently.

To make the difference in your way of interpreting

wealth - and thus giving it some meaning - is the story behind you - your life, your family principles, and in particular your beliefs. Let's start from the experience: if, on your path, you've met rich and "not clever" people (superficial, selfish, dishonest) you have matured a negative image of wealth. You have formulated ideas of the kind: "When you are able to have everything, you don't value anything at all", "if getting rich means to be this way, I prefer to stay as I am," "to make money you have to do something illegal." Or, if you have met poor people who have become enriched and changed at some point, you would have thought that "money transforms people and loses real values."

Likewise, if your father was a great worker but did not make any money despite all his effort, you will come to the conclusion that "work is a sacrifice and does not pay" and, therefore, "you work to survive, not to live "because" work is one thing and dreams are another ".

If you've seen someone having undeserved success because of a stroke of luck, you'll have embraced the idea that "wealth is just a matter of luck." No matter how long that success has been lasting or not!

The convictions bring you to see the reality according to your filter, losing sight of all the rest. When you get stuck in your vision without changing perspective, you do not see things for what they are but for who you are.

If you have matured a negative conception of wealth, you will continue to hold on to it until it does not act against you. Some call it, rightly, self-sabotage.

Italy is in this sense bigoted and inconsistent: Italians love money but hate the rich. It is obvious that there is a bottom line: a contradiction, more or less sub-conscious, that leads to doing everything to achieve a goal (wealth) but, when you are about to get it, it goes backwards (because "Being rich is bad").

You have to make peace with the concept of money. Wealth is any means. It's like a weapon: its function depends on who uses it and it's utility from how it is used.

Likewise, money does not change people; it simply reveals their essence. If today you are a bumblebee with a Fiat and win a Ferrari, tomorrow you will be a bumblebee with a Ferrari. Conversely, those who possess a charismatic and coherent personality will not allow money to make him who is not. One of the problems in dealing with money is the inability to handle it. Wealth has power: to amplify the impact of situations on us. If you're happy, you'll be happier; if you are depressed you will be more depressed.

Money is a tool with which you can get so much but not everything: there is always the point where you are called to deal with yourself and your state of being. And there, you have no excuses.

The truth lies with you and you can only see it. How beautiful it may be and how much it can give you, wealth makes you understand that happiness will al-ways be in your hands and not in your bank account. If you succeed in achieving your dream and earning your business, then you can say, with pride and satisfaction, to be rich and happy.

THE DIFFERENCE BETWEEN HAVING WEALTH AND BEING RICH

This is often confirmed by my successful friend and entrepreneur, Alfio Bardolla. There is a fundamental difference between having wealth and being rich and, precisely, lies in what you can produce from what you already have (or that you do not have).

Let's see what it means, meanwhile, to have wealth. He has wealth who finds himself by inheritance with a capital at his disposal. You have in your hands the fruits of past labor, done by others: grandparents, parents, or other family members.

If money is used but it is not produced, you will sooner or later find yourself in front of a limit: that you can not change the quality of your life because, a priori, there is already a (though substantial) capital to use.

In practice, it is already established how much a year you can spend: there is an annual fixed cost amount beyond which you cannot exceed. It seems like a paradox but it is not. Those who have wealth at some point will have to settle for what they have if they have not been able to increase it.

The real rich person is, instead, the one that generates wealth.

You can start from scratch or a more or less economical base, available. From there you start to generate, by means of what we will soon see, other revenue.

When you produce wealth, you can afford to never settle because you are directly responsible for the quality of your life.

At any time you can decide whether to "do more" in order to earn more, or to slow down to enjoy the full of the money you have accumulated.

Among the two categories (those who have wealth vs. those who are rich), the entrepreneur is placed in the second. When you start a successful business you are destined to produce wealth. Just follow the right moves and think big.

THE FOUR WAYS TO PRODUCE MONEY

Every lifestyle has its own cost and quality. You can say you have a quality life when you produce higher cash than your lifestyle you chose. There are four ways to produce money. No matter how much you need it to do it: to make the difference is the modus operandi you got it with.

To suggest this classification are two great entrepreneurs and economists, Warren Buffet and Donald Trump. Imagine having a piece of paper in front of you and drawing a cross. You will get four squares, arranged on two columns.

In the upper left, find the people who barter their time in exchange for money.

In a certain predetermined time span they do what they know best, or what they are doing, or what they have decided to do in their lives. They can exercise any kind of profession and earn any amount of money but the basic mechanism remains the same. They will always be a hamster in the wheel. They can be waiters, medical luminaries, singers, football players. However, they still have to invest their time in earning skills in exchange for earnings.

In the lower left, there are artisans, that is, those who associate time and money with an idea they have had.

Basically, they had a creative idea, they gave it shape but without a business plan consisting of independent development. For this reason craftsmen also come to high earnings but always at the cost of time. As long as the operation of an idea will depend on you, while having a staff of employees, you will always be the first to have to be behind. It is a challenging and stressful method, where earnings do not pay for fatigue made in psychological and physical terms. So much so that, at times, artisans drop their idea proudly: either because they realize that it is long-term failure or because they come to the conclusion that "stress with disorganization is not worth it."

On the right hand side there are entrepreneurs: they are people who invest an idea together with money in exchange for gains.

If you are a businessman, you are no longer bound to do a job in a given time, because you were first determined to create an automation for which money will come by itself. This is a subtle and complex ability. It's not enough to have luck or to know the right people: you have to put a table, study a plan, see its developments, predict what you can and what you cannot expect.

At first you have to dedicate time, lots of time to it.

Just like you have to believe in it a lot. The projection phase is where you do not earn anything at the moment, but you are so confident that your business will go to the port (and that the money will come) to invest time and energy to it beforehand. You will be paid back for this initial time, later on: after your dream has been set in motion and will automatically start earning.

Then you can say you have generated automatic wealth. You will have more freedom of movement, and without constant presence in the company, you can dedicate yourself to what you want, along with those you want.

Finally, at the bottom right you'll find the investors: they are the ones who invest money to make money. 90% of the population works by following the method of the left column, while only 10% follows the one in the right column. Yet the revenue they generate is reversed: that 90% - who is spending time on money - produces 10% of world wealth, while 10% - who has found a more innovative and automatic way of generating wealth - produces 90%. Isn't it astonishing?

HOW TO GENERATE AUTOMATIC WEALTH

You will be curious at this point to know how automatic wealth is generated. There are three categories of profiles depending on the mode.

The first category is that of investors.

These are people who do not need to invest time to create revenue, from the moment they put their capitals in projects where others work. Investors already have a previous wealth and their ability is to select the projects on which to invest their money. If they have seen it right and the chosen businesses will not fail, they will get a share of those company profits at the end of the year.

The second category is the largest of the three and it is inventors.

They are people who invent a product or service and draw from their mass distribution their revenue and hence the benefits of automatic wealth. This includes writers, singers, creators in general, innovative pharmaceutical patrons, inventors of entertainment and other massive consumer goods.

They are, however, a part of the third category, which is entrepreneurs, like me.

These are the people who create a company devoting ourselves to the beginning of time and energy. So much so that their business plan can then not only stand up without their constant presence but also advance and generate automatic wealth. After elaborating the right business plan, finding the necessary information, selecting the staff and creating a valid professional network, if everything has been done with care and quality, the entrepreneur will just have to do a job of supervising and strategic planning.
A job of supervising, when "the gears of your car"

work, you not require a solid physical presence. This means that you will be able to get out of your car once you have perfected it.

Not only that, while the machine will continue to produce wealth, you can spend the fruits of your work and enjoy your time, rediscovering the full value.

THE FINANCIAL ATTITUDES

Time is the only real resource, it is a value and a variable. Time is the greatest source of wealth.

"Who has time does not wait for time," he says. But beyond time, what else is needed to develop a successful international business? There are those who call it "financial skills", I like to call them "attitudes". These are attitudes that anyone can mature, through the awareness of their own or others' experience.

Financial attitudes represent the ability to deal with time and wealth.

Any quality you have in excess of the average will be useful for you: how to put yourself into play, humility to learn new things by pointing ahead, foresight, and determination ahead of an obstacle.

My gelato chefs, for example, have good financial aptitudes: they have been humble and determined, they have listened to me and are already enjoying the first fruits. From the first day of activity, I had explained the importance of saving 10% of revenue, allocating it and investing it every year. In this way, each year, their money would have increased by 10% compared to gains already matured. Within five years, they could create automatic annuities, equivalent to one year's salary, without any particular sacrifice. Some more enterprising employees have also invested in our gelato shops: there has been one who has asked to take 2% of our shares and is now contributing in his way to the company's economic development. If you know how to convey your financial skills to your employees and employees, you will be the first to benefit. So let yourself be patient with patience and enthusiasm. Inform them, or rather: form them.

THE VALUE OF TIME

Most of the time we talk about time as if it were something that does not belong to us. *"I do not have time," "As soon as I have time I'll do it," "We hope to find time to see each other," "How I would like to have more time."* Time gives, time takes away, time is running away.

Before time you have only one choice: to live your time or to lose it.

Think about the last time you devoted energy to someone or something: Did you ever make a profit after what you had invested? Or did your efforts take time, without repaying you with the same coin? We are used to seeing money as the most precious asset and we lose sight of the only real wealth: our time. Nothing is more than that. Your life is your time. That's why you are called to decide what to do. It is a proper decision that will depend on the quality of your life, yours and your family. Do you want to take up your time continuously, without breaks or spaces of freedom? Lose it behind people, relationships, and wrong work projects? Or do you learn to take your time and give it to people and things that will make it treasure and will they enrich you?

When you create automatic wealth, you are not only producing money but also time. Gain minutes, hours, days, months of freedom you can spend with your loved ones.

All without losing your professional responsibilities. The difference between those who have no time and who has learned to live their time is in the relationship with the latter. If you see time as something that can only be gained from outside, you're more likely to complain that you do not have enough of it than to be able to create it again. If, on the other hand, you can take your time and go out of the dynamic one for which *"I do not have time for me because I have to stay behind the timings of others"* then the ribbon rewinds. Suddenly you not only have time in your hands, but it's as if you were able to earn it again.

Your dream feeds on your time and you, automatically, feed you the same energy: you create a kind of virtuous cycle in which what you are doing and that you make you go back, with more charge than before.

It takes time to learn to stay in time! So do not wait and start now: dedicate yourself to your projects, with confidence, ambition and patience.

CHAPTER 8. THE CONSTANT SEARCH OF HAPPINESS

Practice gratitude every day
and remember to be happy

A flavor for you: Stracciatella
Properties: Simple, rich, genius in its combination. A base of gelato of fiordilatte, mixed with shavings of chocolate. Satisfying and tasty, it's a classic flavor and can't be missed.

THAT CONE OF HAZELNUT GELATO

They say that the happiest moment if that of the finish line, but we usually identify the finish line only in the final part of the journey. At the end of the competition we wait for victory, prize giving and conclusion of the competition, the ranking after the competition. Sometimes we don't enjoy what is before that because we are worried about knowing who will win, what will happen after and why. This goes for when others are in the game, but most of all, when we are in it.

We should, on the other hand, learn to recognize the importance of starts because it is in that ground that we plant the seed of happiness.

Despite the wonderful finish lines that the Gelaterie Versace are reaching today, the happiest moment for me will always be the first day of opening.

I'm not keeping the receipt of that first hazelnut cone by chance. I remember my legs were shaking and enthusiasm was invading my body, mixed adrenaline between courage and fear. Happiness was moving inside of me and everything seemed unreal to me: when your dream takes shape you are so happy to ask yourself if you are really dreaming.

On the contrary, no: we are talking about a wonderful reality that is fed from all the energy that I had invested in it up to this moment. I remember that day, I arrived early to the International Mall and walked in from the back entrance. The protective barricade, the one of work in progress, was gone. It was time to start. Until a few days before I could hear all the noises from behind: the voices of children who were running around the mall, the steps of customers, the noise of neighboring shops.

Now it's all gone. It's like leaning out of the window one morning and realizing that the building that was in front of you until the day before, is suddenly gone. A new different prospective is opening in front of you: a new view, that you can enjoy with new eyes. There is no more fence separating me from my dream, or protecting me from fear.

"Stefano! You made it! Realize that!" – I was thinking.

I overcame all the difficulties and I knew that this would have been the trial day. Or better, the confirmation day. By now I was on the ring and I would have fought until the end: I would have not allowed my dream to fail. As I already told you, the sales were incredible and that day was a conquest: the revenge on my father and other destroyers of dreams, the reward for my wife and for all the support she gave me, the prize of earned happiness, that

finally, I could taste.
"Thank you. Thank you. Thank you. And now, at full throttle!!!"

WHAT IS GRATITUDE

"I am grateful for everything that happened". Or "I am thanking you for everything you did for me". Or, still, a simple but not trivial "thank you from my heart", that we all know well. No one can avoid dealing with gratitude in their lives because there is always something, or someone, who we are grateful for.

The same root of the word refers to the dimension of recognition, and not only. From Sanskrit "gurt-a", from Greek "chart-tos", from Latin "gratitudo": any language you look at , there is a call to everything that is pleasant, jocund, dear to the soul and for that grateful and welcoming. If you think about it, it's exactly what is happening: you are grateful toward something that delights you and contributes to your well-being.

Practicing gratitude means to recognize the benefits obtained from someone, and remembering it.

Generally we identify it with the recognition of power to outside factors: when someone, or something, or any given situation, has a positive influence on our lives we are grateful to that. We thank God for being healthy, fortune for having us given that chance we can't miss, the partner for being supportive, the family for the education they gave us.

The most extraordinary type of gratitude remains, however, the one you have toward yourself.

When you recognize in you, before others or external circumstances do, the capacity to get better, you gain in power. In that moment you express the conviction of being determinant for your life: even if you don't have the control (it would be useless and impossible), you have influence on it. To manage your own life, planning any unforeseen circumstance and acting only with reason, isn't part of the human dimension: there are unforeseen events, relationships that transform you, and in that sense, changes that you can't avoid.

A chines proverb goes:

"When the wind of change blows, there is who is building walls, and who is building windmills."

When you give yourself the power to influence your life, it's as if you are building windmills. You welcome change but you manage it based on your resources and potential. And not only. To be grateful toward yourself mean also motivating yourself to reach your goals.

You know that all you need is inside of you. You just have to find it, but you know it's there.

And so gratitude feeds self respect and becomes also a personal power: it's the incentive to reach the finish line. Or better, to reach success. You can't take decisions for someone else, neither have complete control over your life: but you can manage yourself better and choose how to deal with it.

When you practice gratitude you are also working on your awareness.

The thankful person is the person who realized of what they can give of themselves to others.

At the same time it is also the person who can recognize the gifts given and the help offered. Gratitude is based on a good relationship with yourself, and with others.

YOUR RELATIONSHIPS ARE PRECIOUS

Don't underestimate the power of your relationships. They are not the wheel of your ship, but are however great travel companions. Especially those dear to you. The power to decide what to do with your life is always up to you. But to know that you have someone close to you, while you make decisions, makes the difference. I'm talking about those times where change blows strong and suddenly, and the closeness of someone dear to you can alleviate a temporary tension. I'm talking about the support that the person who loves you is able to give to you, when you need a should to lean on and with whom to relate.

Your relationships are precious and need to be fed, every day, giving all you can.

Don't take them for granted: nobody is forced to stay in your life forever, unless you want it with all your being. Train yourself to be aware of who is giving you love, strength and support.
Gratitude towards others is essential also to keep doors open in the future, which otherwise could shut. Think, for example, when someone is helping you in some situation

but doesn't feel appreciated because you are not even saying "thank you". In that moment you are depriving yourself from a future chance of getting more support from him. When on the other hand you are grateful and show a sincere appreciation, your relations become more solid, connected and open. Not just those close to you, but also professional ones.

You elaborate and set the bases of success, but success itself you will reach with team work.

If you don't have a good relationship with your team, if you don't trust your coworkers (and you are not trustworthy yourself), you won't be able to build an effective net of contacts, and you will inevitably find more difficulty on the road of success.
Every day I turn to thank all the people who are contributing to the realization of my dream. The passion my employees have while working needs to be rewarded: in that way you avoid that one day they will wake up and tell themselves "but why am I working without being appreciated?". By thanking your staff you will motivate them and stimulate them even more.

Nothing is owed to you: even when you deserve something, be grateful that this happened to you.

SAY NO TO VICTIMHOOD AND GUILTY FEELINGS

There are people who are not grateful towards others or themselves, and even feel guilty. It's an attitude one can have once in a while. When one thing after the other happens to you, you ask yourself: *"what did I do to deserve this?"* Or, if everything you built – a solid relationship, your business, property – it suddenly falls apart, and you start asking yourself the wrong questions. "Why me?, "Why is God punishing me?", "What is my destiny trying to tell me?", "What sense is there in going on fighting?", "Why is everything gone that I care about?".

As you have learned by now, a low quality question deserves a low quality answer, that in itself generates convictions and behaviors that are destructive and not efficient.

Asking yourself the wrong questions, you are not only thinking negatively about what is happening to you, but also about yourself. In that moment you forget all the good you have done in the past and you enter a vicious circle, where you are looking for answers that don't make any sense.

When you make a mistake, when the inevitable happens or an unexpected event ruins plans, there are other questions to ask.

Train yourself to think in a constructive way. To pity yourself, play the victim and blame yourself when facing adversities, are reactions that are looking for consolations… instead for the solution of a certain problem. The intelligent questions are different: "What can I do to better the situation?", "What and whom can I influence?", "How can I make a first step to change the situation?". So you move the attention from feelings of guilt to a possible solution, and you are getting your power back.

Watch out though.

Not feeling guilty doesn't mean to stop being critical toward oneself.

Healthy criticism is good, if you do it yourself, or when others criticize you: your own performance will get better and tests relationships. You understand that you can trust someone, when he is ready to criticize you in a constructive way. The right way is to find the reasons why something went wrong and didn't go by the plans: the mistake is to fossilize on the mistakes!

Not blaming oneself doesn't meant to stop blaming yourself in order to give blame to the others.

It would be much better at this point to find a responsibility than a fault.
Always take responsibility – and not fault – of your actions.
Remember that every mistake has positive fruits inside of it: you just need to pick them and find out what to do to better yourself.

HAPPINESS AS A BALANCE

When you become aware of your resources, you reach your goals, practice gratitude and cultivate solid and rewarding relationships, you can say to be finally happy. A lot of people see happiness as something ephemeral: some sort of moment to seize, an emotional status to enjoy because it will disappear shortly. In reality, happiness is exactly the opposite: it's not necessarily something exciting, or an illumination, or a perennial condition of equability.

Happiness is balance: you are happy when you are in harmony with your expectations, your reached goals, your relationships and what is around you.

When you feel satisfied from a health, economical, relational and affective point of view, then you can say to be happy. When what you give – and are willing to give – corresponds with what you are willing to receive, then there is an exchange, there is nourishment, there is happiness. The trick is to not throw off the balance the plate of the scale. Think, for example, of a relationship where one of the two loves the other twice as much: there will be off balances and absences that will lead to unhappiness, rather than an affectionate fulfillment.
When you go beyond your expectations, or vice versa, you stop before, you feel uncomfortable. There is no relation between what you thought would make you happy and what, in fact, you achieved.

For happiness to exist there must be alignment.

It's as if you were a millionaire and went on vacation with a worker: every time that you spend huge amounts of money, compared to spending capacities of the other, you will inevitably feel uncomfortable. Happiness doesn't mean to flatten yourself on the level offered to you, but to feel in harmony and balance with your way of being. To not settle could be a future reason for unhappiness, but also to settle is: all depends on you on what you desire and how much are aware of it.

Happiness is a private emotion: only you know what makes you happy and only you can recognize and feel the effects of happiness inside of you.

Sometimes we confuse the display of happiness with happiness itself: "If you are happy, show it and tell the world!": who says that there is a need to show off happiness? The risk is there to end of pretending with yourself. There are people who are not happy but convince themselves of being happy, sharing their apparent bliss with others. What some people do on social networks is an example of that. Think of those couples who fill their facebook wall with pictures "we are the perfect family" style, but who, once you know them in real life, don't show any happiness. Or who wants to give an idea of a successful and fulfilled person and says things *ad hoc* simply to get compliments from others.

The real sharing is what comes from the heart, instead of the head. It's not a strategy, it's a natural being. So sharing happiness become an authentic gesture and not a manipulative one. Sharing is ok but is remains an emotional amplifier: happiness is an internal sentimental status. If it's not there, you don't feel it, and you can't amplify it.

HOW HAPPY DO YOU WANT TO BE?

Nobody is obliged to feel happy. Happiness is a right, not a duty. Ask yourself honestly and answer freely: "who happy do I want to be?".

If you are not the first one wanting and fighting for your happiness, nobody can do it for you.

To have your life depend on someone else's is senseless and generates, in the long run, unhappiness. Only you know what can really make you happy and how to draw your resources to obtain it. We are the workshop of our own happiness: others can help us, share resources, offer us constructive ideas but the strongest power is the one that we have (because we are talking about our happiness, not theirs!).

Happiness is a conquest that requires to affirm oneself, every day.

Determination, tenacity, authenticity and willingness are needed. Talent by itself is not enough. You are reaching happiness when you go forward and know what you want, regardless of the obstacles that are between you and your objective. Think about some soccer players that have "scarce feet" but an impressionable tenacity: those are the ones that end up in the World Cup and are speeding across the field, unlocking an ability that you would have never expected from their physical structure. I met talented people who got lost on their way because they didn't have a flame inside. That ardor that pushes you, every time you fall, in order to get back up and fight even stronger than before.

Success is the persistent and constant search for happiness.

There has to be continuity: you have to work on it every day and built that tassel that feeds your future, and the one of your loved ones.
Clearly believing in yourself is fundamental: no one chases something if he thinks that he doesn't deserve it or that

he is not able to get it. Take care of your passion, trust your talent and remember, every day, to be happy: happiness is built step by step.

THE CONNECTION BETWEEN SUCCESS AND LOVE

If you don't know how to love you will never be able to be successful. If you don't love life, yourself, your family, your job, you will never be so determined to feed that fire inside of you for a long time. Love is the motor of your existence.

Time is the real resource of wealth, love is the first source of energy.

When you love something, someone, an idea, you dedicate your time and invest the maximum of your energy. You give a lot and you get a lot: that's why you can't help being grateful.
We have arrived to the end of this book but my journey will continue, just like yours. Don't forget to thank who you love, for everything they have done for you. These may seem obvious words but what is left is what you pass on, not what you possess.

You transmit love, you don't possess it. When you open yourself up to love, you get so much energy from it that you feel able to fight for anything.

So I am thanking love for having entered my life and having given me happiness. In particular, I am thanking three people, grouped in two: my wife Carolina and my wonderful sons. Before an entrepreneur, I am a husband and father. Without them I wouldn't be here, as I am now.

Thank you Carolina for being the love of my life. How much you have supported me and endured me, my love. Even when everything went wrong, you found the force to smile and didn't make me feel like a burden. You lightened my mistakes, because you wanted to share them with me without expecting anything in return, if not to see me happy. As I am, as we are today.

Many couples flake off when things start to be shaky, because it's always easier to love when things go well. It's when the earthquake hits that you see how strong you feel for someone. I remember when we were lived in poverty in Venezuela and money was spent to feed our son. I remember when you were looking at me and in your eyes there was everything: love, comfort, courage, understanding. Everything but hostility, friction, judgement. You never asked me to give up or to throw away my dream. You hugged every possibility that I found in front of me because you always trusted me. As I trusted you.

In these difficult times our love strengthened and now we are anchored, connected, one to the other. You are my sun, Carolina.

And then there are our children. The fruits of our love, and at the same time, the source of our love. We gave birth to them, and from the first year of their lives, we gave them the possibility of experimenting what travel meant. The first one was born in a south American country: as soon as he started speaking Spanish, we uprooted him and brought him to Italy. When he got used to living in Italy we left for America. The little one had the same agility of growing.

Our children grew up "flying". Physically and metaphorically. They were always ready for change, new and unexpected things. They are open to exchanges, diversities, confrontations. They have a high capacity of interaction and a predisposition to social contact. Sometimes we get to the beach and don't even have time to sit down, when they are already playing with friends they met just a minute ago!

Today in our house we speak three languages and there are no arguments of "strange" dialogue, that we are not interested in. The world is the big common subject. But the most beautiful thing is their look: they look at us with eyes full of love and gratitude. As if they were saying: "Thank you mom and dad for all the love that you are giving to us. For all the love that is there."

Blessed is this life and happiness that brought us here.

The day I married my wife, together with the birth of my sons, will be unbreakable moments in my heart. As soon as they came into my life, one at the time, I made a step forward every day. Toward happiness, toward a new dimension: that of love, success and the union that binds us. My dear reader who followed me up to here: the time has come to say goodbye. I hope that you have learned enough from this book: the necessary juice to feed your dream. Remember that every success is possible, if you act with love, gratitude, competence and creativity.

Create then, your success starting from you, but do it with all the love that is there with the support of your loved ones by your side. You will not fail, if you won't allow it.

Happy search for happiness: start from today.
Every moment is the right one: let the future start from here.

Table of Contents

Translation by Silvia Bertolazzi